PRAISE FOR
Taking Baghdad

"USMC Veteran Aaron Michael Grant's account of *Taking Baghdad* is a gripping true-life narrative of an event not to be repeated in our lifetime. If you only read one book on the Iraq invasion THIS IS IT!

—COMMAND SERGEANT MAJOR DENNIS WOODS, author of *Black Flag Journals*

"This is a surprisingly candid inside look at going to war. From boredom to the battlefield, Aaron Grant has done a superb job of transporting the reader to the buildup and invasion into Iraq. I could feel the heat, the sand in my eyes, and taste the fear. His easy and readable style coupled with his poetry, prose and pictures make this an interesting journey to travel with him. *Taking Bagdad* is as real and gritty as it gets. I found it an interesting blend of battlefield realities and the inner battle of a decent man in engaged in a 'total war.' His coming home chapter is every veteran's story. This should be required reading for anyone who even thinks about sending our men and women into war. It is terrible and exciting, heart-breaking and inspirational."

—THOMAS PAUL REILLY, author of *Hope in The Shadows of War*

"*Taking Baghdad* is a first-hand account of a US Marine who participated in the Iraq War and the taking of Baghdad. Grant's writing highlights his time in Iraq, but moreover it is a display of humanity in the midst of the most trying circumstances a soldier can endure. Grant's personal journal entries document these experiences and, undoubtedly, mirror those emotions and challenges of other American warriors. The minute details, like apricots and Willie offer the reader an insight few have written on. Grant further illustrates the differences between those who embrace democracy (U.S.) and those with no true understanding of the notion. Grant writes, 'We forced freedom on a people that had not risen up to claim it themselves.' (p. 101) Similarly, the human element is displayed in his writing of fathers willing to give up their daughters to the US Marines in hopes they all escape to America where they will be free and not pawns, victims, and more. Grant's writing takes you there —you are experiencing firsthand the trials and tribulations of war, as well as the sweet taste of victory. You understand what the Iraqi people endured under Saddam's evil regime both during the conflict and the immediate aftermath of the fall of Baghdad.

"A well written and documented account. A must read for those who truly want to know what the war was like and all that that entailed—the good, the bad, and the ugly."

—DR. DAVID L. HARMON, Professor of History, University of Maryland, University College

"Aaron Grant has written an especially vivid and insightful war memoir. It deserves wide reading."

—DR. ANDREW J. BLACEVICH, Professor of History Emeritus, Boston University. Winner of the American Book Award. Author of *Americas War for the Greater Middle East*

Taking Baghdad:
Victory in Iraq with the US Marines

by Aaron Michael Grant

© Copyright 2019 Aaron Michael Grant

ISBN 978-1-63393-793-2

All rights reserved. No part of this publication may be reproduced, stored in a retrieval system, or transmitted in any form or by any means—electronic, mechanical, photocopy, recording, or any other—except for brief quotations in printed reviews, without the prior written permission of the author.

Published by

210 60th Street
Virginia Beach, VA 23451
800-435-4811
www.koehlerbooks.com

TAKING BAGHDAD

VICTORY IN IRAQ WITH THE US MARINES

AARON MICHAEL GRANT

VIRGINIA BEACH
CAPE CHARLES

To my Children

My Treasure

And to the Veteran

My Brothers

CONTENTS

Preface 6

Chapter I: The Marine and the Man 11

Chapter II: Surviving Kuwait 23

Chapter III: Invading Iraq 60

Chapter IV: Everything Changes 87

Chapter V: The Nature of our War 95

Chapter VI: The Cloverleaf and the Night of Mortars 106

Chapter VII: Hells Wrecker Dies 153

Chapter VIII: Taking Baghdad 166

Chapter IX: Home 187

Epilogue: My Time in the Woods 192

In Memoriam 203

Presidential Citation 204

Regimental Combat Team (Reinforced) 206

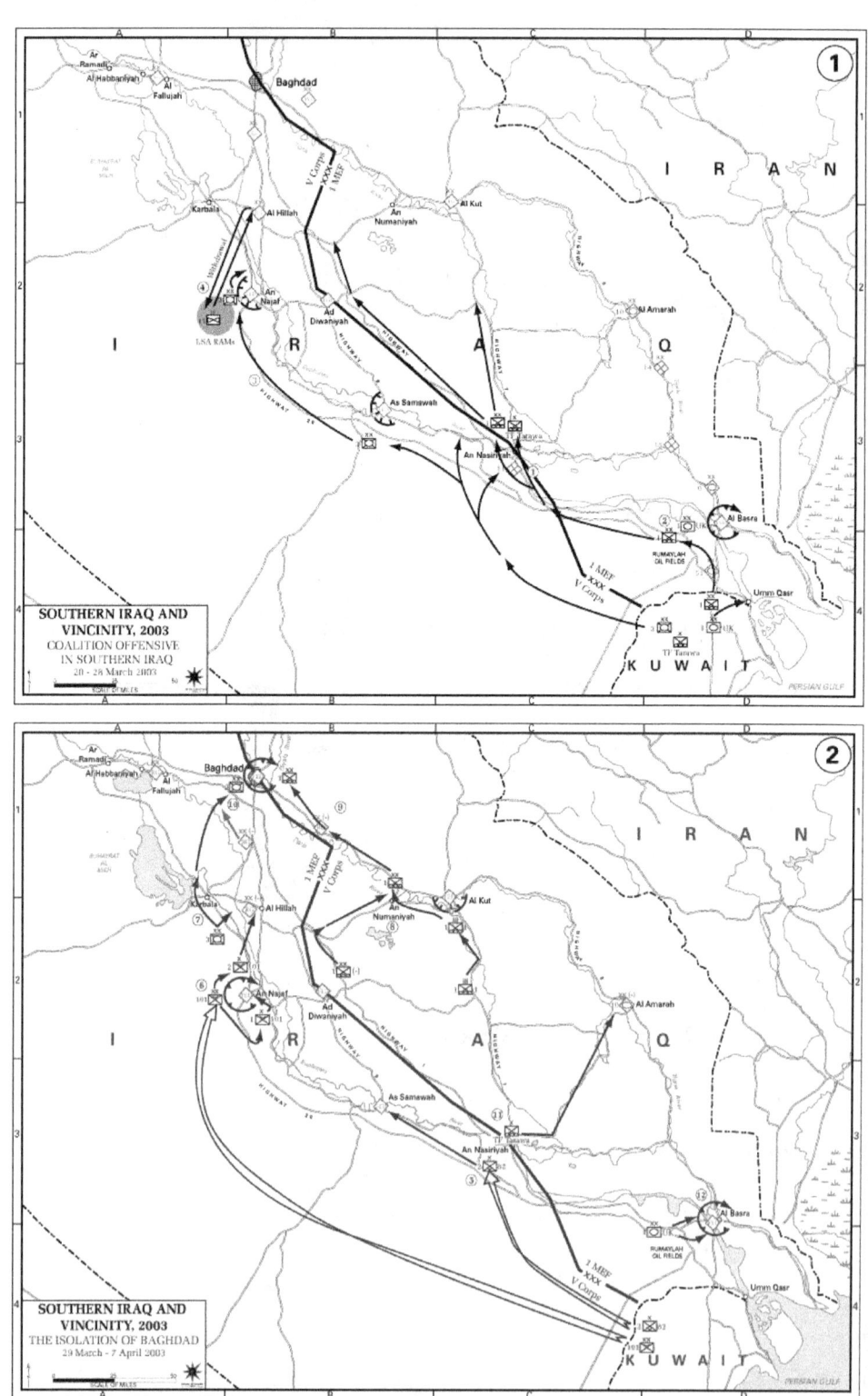

OPERATION IRAQI FREEDOM
TABLE OF SYMBOLS
BASIC SYMBOLS

Team / Crew	ø	Coalition Unit	▢
Squad	•	Saddam Regime / Insurgent Unit	◇
Section	••	Infantry	✕
Platoon	•••	Armor / Mechanized	○
Company / Battery / Troop	I	Motorized / Stryker	∞
Battalion / Squadron	II	Cavalry / Reconnaissance, Surveillance, Target Acquisiton	╱
Regiment / Regimental Combat Team	III	Artillery	●
Brigade	x	Aviation	⋈
Division	xx	Engineer	⊓
Corps / Marine Expeditionary Force	xxx	Airborne	⋎
Republican Guard Element	RG	Air Assault	⌣
Saddam Fedayeen Irregulars	FED	Marine Corps	⋒
Al Qaeda in Iraq Insurgents	AQI	Special Operations Forces	SF
Jaysh Al Mahdi Insurgents	JAM	British Unit	UK
Unknown Insurgent Group	IN	Iraq Army / Police - Post Saddam	IA/IP

EXAMPLE of COMBINATIONS of BASIC SYMBOLS

3rd Infantry Division (Mechanized) .... 3[○̷]

101st Infantry Division (Air Assault) .... 101[⌣̷]

2nd Brigade, 82nd Airborne Division .... 2[⋎̷]82

1st Regimental Combat Team, 1st Marine Division .... 1[⋒̷]1

1st British Armored Division .... 1[○]UK

Iraqi 51st Mechanized Infantry Division .... 51[◇̷○]
(Saddam Hussein Regime)

Fedayeen Irregular (Size Unknown) .... ◇

OTHER SYMBOLS

MISSION SYMBOLS:

Clear: Mission to remove all enemy forces and eliminate organized resistance in assigned area .... ↑↑↑

Contain: Mission to stop, hold, or surround enemy forces .... ↻

Isolate: Mission that requires a unit to seal off - both physically and psychologically - an enemy from his sources of support, deny an enemy freedom of movement, and prevent an enemy unit from having contact with other enemy forces .... ⊃

Secure: Mission that involves preventing a geographic location from being damaged or destroyed as a result of enemy action .... ↺

Withdrawal: A planned operation in which a force in contact disengages from an enemy force .... ——→

Unit Boundary (Corps Boundary) .... ——— xxx ———

Credit: West Point History Department. http://www.usma.edu

PREFACE

THIS WAS IT. It was either go to war for America, or desert like a coward. I lay curled up on the floor debating. They didn't teach us to be patriots; they didn't make us go when our country called. It was a decision of the man to heed the call. Freedom. Precious freedom.

The US Marine Corps taught me to defend freedom—the Constitution. The Corps taught me how to fight, taught me to be without fear, but here I was, gasping for air as if it were my last moment on earth. If I deserted, it would be a crime against the men who served with me. Yet, I longed for freedom. Freedom from responsibility.

I didn't want to kill Iraqis. What had they ever done to me? Could I shoot Saddam Hussein? Could I shoot anybody? I was a noncommissioned officer, a corporal, which stood for something. Marines served under me and my leaders depended upon me. I was somebody. Especially to my family. My precious family. I was their representative in the oncoming war. My talents, my blunders, my quality was theirs. Could I abandon my men? Could I taint my family's name?

An ancestor of mine once took that road. In 1860, a young Scotch immigrant named Peter Grant came to America and enlisted in the Army. He didn't plan for a war. He was trained to fight, but he lacked the courage to stand with his brothers. He came down with influenza—that's what the records say—and after the fever and diarrhea, and God knows how many sleepless nights, he was racked with the decision to either desert or serve in the war with the Southern states.

The wretched illness leveled him, and what, being a mere private, would make a difference if he stayed or deserted? He had no men to command, only men to serve, to fight beside, to protect. What caused him to leave I will never know. But while ill he decided to cast away his uniform and obligation to his friends. He slipped away, probably at night dressed as a civilian, and made a harrowing journey to the north, to Canada, beyond the reach of the federal government. There he stayed, a deserter and a disgrace, not just to his family but to himself. Some in the family said they didn't blame him, but most knew the cold truth—he was a coward. Did he ever rise above his disgrace? Did it even matter?

It mattered to me in 2003. As I lay there on the floor, I became keenly aware that my family was watching. Some came to see what was wrong, and in that moment when the eyes were upon me, I decided. I would fight, dammit. I was to represent the hopes and dreams of those who did not take my oath but who depended upon it. I would not disgrace them as Peter had. I don't know if they saw the change in me, but I stood with a renewed sense of purpose. I stood for them. I stood for myself. I was a United States Marine and I could conquer the whole earth.

"Fear is a reaction, courage is a decision."

WINSTON CHURCHILL

CHAPTER I

THE MARINE AND THE MAN

THIS STORY BEGINS IN the woods, opposite the desert in all respects. Green, full of life, encasing me in solitude to rid myself, even if temporarily, the reality of life. I went there as a child to escape, and now, as a man with a title and an obligation to the Marine Corps, I walked aimlessly ruminating, head in the canopy of leaves, completely at home. This was to be my last walk in peace before the war. I would soon be called to participate in a new kind of war in Iraq, and as I remembered lying on the floor, I was afraid no more. Somehow, I knew I would live to return to America. Something in my conscience, God, assured me I would return. In that I found comfort, and I focused on Him for the moment, for soldiers lean on God.

It happened in the woods. I fell to my knees and prayed, hands clasped. I wish I could remember the words. They elude me, but they were the most delicate, meaningful sentiments of my young life as a Christian. I was young, and I didn't know everything about God, or the Bible, but I needed Him, and, in faith, what I said was true, from the heart, and lasting. Time slowed as I gave it my all. The flap of a bird's wings, the wind through the trees, the sound of squirrels rustling in the leaves. I listened, pausing between the words, and before long dusk opened my eyes. The stars were already overhead, and as I exhaled the crisp January air, I felt God in the night. Arm in arm, we spoke as I left the woods ready—sure of myself, sure of my survival. My soul was complete; nothing could stop me.

As an NCO, I was responsible for the training and discipline of those beneath me and taking the orders of those above me. I had only been enlisted for two years, and after boot camp at Parris Island, South Carolina, and tank mechanic school in Fort Knox, Kentucky, I joined Bravo Company, 2nd Tank Battalion, 2nd Marine Division out of Camp Lejeune, North Carolina. I was a rookie, a "boot," as short-timers were called, and I was expert with a rifle, outstanding in Marine Corps knowledge, and most of all ambitious.

A drill instructor once told me that I would rise quickly through the ranks, and I aimed to do just that. A youth, I was still without glory. Sure, becoming a Marine was important enough, but I was inexperienced, not a war veteran like the staff and field officers that would command me. I had not made my mark on history—yet. I was determined that I would serve with honor, if not with distinction, because all the chips were on the table. I would not retreat back home dishonored. I would come back with my rifle or beneath it.

I left the woods with my thoughts, as it was time to take orders. I had never killed a man and had not thought much of it until this instant. Could I do it? For the right cause, yes. I convinced myself I would have the courage to pull the trigger, but when it came down to it, I did not know how I would react to deadly force. Trained in the wilderness of Parris Island, my heart was a soldier's heart from the time I was trained to fire a rifle, to throw a grenade, to crawl under barbed wire. I was motivated, though I did not know how to transfer that motivation to others. Through it all, though, the training was make-believe. The rounds they fired were blanks, the stress they imposed was fake, and the maneuvers we practiced were safe. I had never feared for my life, though I was surrounded by senior Marines who had. Our superiors did not talk of their wars: the Gulf War, Kosovo, and Granada. They should have, for we might have learned how to conquer fear from them—to be better fighters. Better Marines.

Camp Lejeune was afire with activity. The olive-drab platoons ran and trained in the darkness, in the rain, in the mud. They all knew war was coming, and the ambitious officers and NCOs prepared and drilled them hard. Chin over that pull-up bar; lie on the dewy grass and destroy the abdomen with sit-ups; and a three-mile run to top it off. Men puked after they gave it their all. A good running time was anything under twenty minutes. And it didn't stop there.

As I was driving back to barracks, I knew I had to set the example, keeping abreast of the preparations, and take my sergeant's orders. This would be the last ride in my Jeep, top down and the wind in my hair, pretending to be carefree and looking at the stars confident that I knew what was coming.

Military history judges not only war and the manner in which it was fought; it also judges how a military force is trained and its application of training in war. The Marines are nothing if not meticulous, and their constant preparation for combat makes them the best invasion force America can muster. So much information about a military is lost when one does not take into account the preparation for war; even mundane facts measure the outcome of battles. It's the small things that count. Every man with pride in his gear, pride in his equipment, pride in his unit, esprit de corps, is exactly the force needed to shock the enemy and destroy their will to fight. Every detail measures the outcome of war, down to each Marine and his unit.

In order to be properly prepared for deployment, all gear had to be accounted for. This meant ruthless, relentless, even pointless inspections of everything from personal hygiene gear to SL-3 gear for the tanks—all equipment every tank needed to deploy, such as a track jack known as a "dog-bone," extra track pads, and even massive jumper cables. This was the way the Marine Corps did things, and it did not stop with 2nd Tank Battalion. Every Marine on Camp Lejeune was frantically buying up items he did not have to pass inspection, such as socks, baby wipes (for something we called a "field shower"), and Aqua Velva.

Issued gear included helmets, ALICE packs, and gun-cleaning gear. Marines without these essentials would get written up. It was surprisingly common for a Marine to have something like a helmet go missing, and he would be a fool to show up to inspection without it, so he bought a replacement either off-base or from the black market of used gear that permeated Camp Lejeune and, to be fair, all US military bases abroad. Every Marine knew some other Marine who could "get things" for a fee. The end result was a common saying in the Corps: "There are no thieves in the Marine Corps, just Marines trying to get their shit back."

Preparations included a slew of anthrax vaccinations. The 2nd Tank Battalion was rounded up to the gymnasium just outside the barracks and briefed that all Marines and sailors, including the officers, would get an anthrax vaccination because the Iraqi dictator Saddam Hussein was rumored to have anthrax chemical weapons. Our commanding officer, Lieutenant Colonel Michael J. Oehl, along with his sergeant major, stated that the vaccine was *required* for deployment—though, officially, getting it was *optional*. The recourse was an automatic non-judicial punishment (NJP) if one decided not to take it. An NJP could destroy a Marine's prospects of getting promoted in a timely fashion and was a permanent scar to careerists. So, with the threat deeply rooted in our minds, the Marines universally lined up to take the anthrax vaccine, even though it was experimental and rumored to have side effects. We felt we had no choice. My arm still carries the scar of two rounds of the vaccine, and I explicitly remember some Marines puking immediately after they received the shot. Others who had seizures or heart attacks were *quietly* discharged for medical reasons.[1] In the end I wished I had not taken the shot, though I did not share that sentiment with others.

The entire battalion was also put through the fabled "gas chamber" as part of its pre-deployment preparations. The battalion's nuclear, biological, and chemical defense (NBCD) section gave classes on how to suit up in MOPP gear—mission oriented protective posture. The military issued special uniforms in the event of a chemical attack to every Marine, including a rubber-and-charcoal-lined suit, rubber gloves and boots, and a gas mask. We suited up outside the chamber filled with green smoke until we all resembled chemical workers sucking air through our masks. Single-file, we entered the cement room and stood back to the wall, facing the center fire of CS (chlorobenzalmalononitrile) riot control tear gas. The door was closed. To show us that our masks were working properly, an officer at the center of the room yelled, "OFF MASKS! REMOVE YOUR MASKS!" We all obeyed. Within a minute we were choking on the pepper-like fumes. My nose dripped like a faucet; my eyes, closed, burned and teared. A few Marines doubled over, vomiting as we stood in place. All were suffering, and the Marine at the center of the chamber got his jollies watching the horrid scene. After he was satisfied, he yelled, "DON MASKS! DON MASKS!" The Marines immediately replaced their masks tightly and blew air out the seals, allowing clean oxygen to fill their lungs. Still coughing as the door was opened, the Marines quickly exited the chamber in single-file. There is no greater sense of relief than exiting a gas chamber. I survived the chamber many times, and it never got easier.

Nighttime at the barracks meant time to drink. Marines love to drink anything and everything, and we all knew we were to be deployed soon. Marines under the influence were doing stupid things, playing video games, and preparing for the next inspection. Everyone had his ritual. The NCOs stuck together, and so did the

---

1   Recollections of Cpl. Alan Bartlow, a Marine in 2nd Battalion, 6th Marines stationed at Camp Lejeune, N.C. at the time of the Anthrax shots.

troops of lesser rank. Fraternization was not allowed between troops and NCOs, so when a man was promoted above the rank of lance corporal he had to disconnect from his friends and assume a new yoke. The corporals and sergeants hung together on one end of the barracks and the troops occupied the rest. Late into the night the two would sometimes mix and hazing would commence. Fights and silly games ensued.

The night before we deployed I decided to hit a troop in the crotch; it was all in good fun, so he punched me in the head. A true Marine never told what happened the night before when he was standing at attention in formation. He shut his mouth; what happened at the barracks stayed at the barracks.

We were given a little time the day before deploying to take care of personal business. For some, that meant seeing family, automating payment plans, or storing cars for the year to come. I was ready save for one thing. I had to dump my girlfriend before leaving for Iraq. I told her I could not focus otherwise. I was sort of a pro at going through girlfriends by 2003, and besides, it was not true love. I was saving that for someone else. So, it was over between her and me, and thank God I had the foresight to do it. I had to focus all on battle or nothing at all. I could not have one foot in America and the other on the ground in Iraq. To do so would have gotten me killed, and I see that today. I went to Iraq alone save my familial support, and honestly I would have it no other way.

★ ★ ★ ★ ★

The next morning, when we had all our gear packed, I began to think about Operation Iraqi Freedom. It was not to be like that last war in Iraq, where the majority of casualties were caused by the US Air Force and Saddam Hussein was simply trying to invade Kuwait. Now, twelve years later, a massive buildup of American forces gathered in northern Kuwait and other border nations. The Marine Corps, Army, Air Force, and Coast Guard with allied troops from Britain, Australia, and Poland flexed their muscles at the Iraq-Kuwait border. And why? Because Saddam Hussein was said to be hiding chemical weapons off in the desert. He would not reveal them to the United Nations' inspectors, even knowing that everybody knew he used them in the Iran-Iraq War and against the Kurds in Northern Iraq. Mustard gas was his favorite because it was cheap and effective, causing large blisters on the skin and in the lungs of the unfortunate human target. The dictator repeatedly refused to allow UN inspectors access to his chemical weapons facilities.

President George W. Bush was unable to convince the UN to enforce its policies with military action. So, in 2002 he turned to a preemptive form of defense. In what is now known as the Bush Doctrine, the president strongly advocated that America must anticipate attacks upon its borders and therefore strike out at terrorism before it had the chance to harm Americans. "Responding to such enemies only after they have struck is not self-defense, it is suicide," the president stated March 17, 2003, immediately before the US-led force crossed the southern border of Iraq to oust its regime.

Regardless of doctrine, it seemed to me and many of the Marines that we were being deployed because of 9/11. The terrorist attack on our soil in New York and the Pentagon was fresh in all minds. To make it worse, Al Qaeda and Osama Bin Laden claimed the victory, but they were hidden in the mountains of Afghanistan, and in other terrorist-harboring nations like Pakistan and Iran. I thought of the adage, "When there's blood on the streets, someone's got to hang." In this case, it appeared that Saddam was going to hang for hiding his weapons of mass destruction and harboring terrorists like Al Qaeda. So, we were going after him with the greatest, most advanced military ever, and my unit, Bravo Company 2nd Tank Battalion, was soon to be in the spotlight.

Clearly in our minds was that September morning in 2001. I was a private first class then and knew nothing about my own job, much less what was going on in world affairs. That day started like any other.

After a grueling workout in the morning, I dragged my feet to the worst duty anyone could hold—phone watch. I sat in the office surrounded by sergeants and officers and took their orders like I was under a microscope. *Better not crack a smile on phone watch*, I thought, sitting stiff like I was in the electric chair. Then it all changed. The phone erupted with wives and sweethearts calling in. "Is everything okay down there?" they asked. I replied that it was before turning on the TV.

Before I knew it, everyone important was in the office and I was answering the phone like mad. I chanced to look up to the screen and saw a plane fly into the World Trade Center. I was shocked. We all were. And the silence of all the men in uniform, all the tough Marines, canceled out the ringing. It was all I could do to keep my bearing. Then a tower collapsed. "Oh my God! What?!" Dumbfounded, I was sure it wasn't real. *The building shouldn't have fallen like that!* Then another fell, capsizing in dust that cascaded throughout the city. *This can't be happening!* Officers finally got over the shock and began mustering their scattered platoons. I sat staring and met the eyes of a sergeant in the room.

"Get ready," he said. "We're going to war."

It was time to get serious. I focused on my platoon of tanks—headquarters, leading three combat platoons of yet more tanks. Each company contained four platoons, each in 2nd Tank Battalion, and had thirteen combat-ready M1-A1 Abrams tanks supported by a maintenance crew with the M-88 Hercules Tank Retriever, and an obscure advanced vehicular lift bridge (AVLB) with their respective crews. Fifteen massive tanks and tracked vehicles were the responsibility of a small maintenance crew of approximately ten Marines, and I was one of that crew. On a chalkboard in our office at the "tank ramp" was a list of all of the tanks in our company and their problems, from a single cable to entire systems like the gunner's station and the commander's cupola. The list went on and on. There was always more work than could be done on the tanks. Part of the problem was that there was a slim budget for replacement parts due to Clinton-era military cutbacks, and only the most important items would get replaced. As a result, all of the tanks had jerry-rigged parts to keep them combat-ready. They looked impressive on the surface, but in truth they were an absolute disaster for mission readiness.

Every maintenance crew in the battalion begged, borrowed, and stole parts to keep their tanks ready. Some were more successful than others; for example, Charlie (C) Company was renowned for their mysterious reserve of tank parts only accessible to them under lock and key. Sometimes a maintenance crew chief from a neighboring company would send out one of the troops to pay homage to Charlie Company in order to get a part. No one knew what they had, but Charlie had it all. I was sent out on many occasions, directed to find a way to fix a tank, and would stop by buddies in Charlie Company to see if they could help me. Most of the time they were stingy and I would end up making friendships in another company to get the parts I needed. Everyone knew the source of Charlie's wealth; they simply stole the parts from down tanks, either outgoing to get refurbished or at their neighbor's expense. I could not blame them. They were just trying to survive, like Bravo Company. Every tank mechanic had to be resourceful on the extant black market to be considered a good mechanic. I was a Marine of integrity, so naturally I was the worst mechanic on the tank ramp because I could not fix tanks with stolen parts. I am not exaggerating; the state of our federal budget made us that way.

Preparing for deployment was no small task to a tank mechanic. Every maintenance crew in the company was given a quadcon—a huge metal storage crate—to fill with their spare parts and sensitive equipment. It was full of parts we thought we would need in Iraq, some of which we should not have had, according to the books. Bravo Company's crate was quite empty compared to others, which would come to haunt us later in the war.

On top of storing our gear and fixing all our problems, we had another behemoth to worry about. That was the M-88-A2 named

"Hells Wrecker." Months before, the Bravo Company maintenance chief made a mental note that Corporal Aaron Grant was the only marine in the maintenance crew that truly cared for the vehicle. I did all the semi-annual and annual maintenance of Hells Wrecker mostly by myself. I wanted a tank all to myself, and the closest I could get to that was the M-88-A2. I cleaned the air filters, replaced the seals, greased the fittings, cleaned the floors, and maintained the track in my spare time. In his wisdom, the maintenance chief named me one of the crew in the months before Iraq.

My task, as well as that of the other two Marines in the crew, was to recover damaged or malfunctioning tanks—not only the M1-A1 Abrams, but literally anything that got mired; tanks, tracked vehicles, Humvees, and trucks, the crew would release them from the mud to provide the utilities and raw pulling power to recover anything on the battlefield. I spent many months in the fields of Camp Lejeune training to do just that.

Without the sleek lines of a M1-A2 Abrams, Hells Wrecker is truly ugly. A plough (spade) in the front can be used to move earth; above it, the front slopes steeply vertical, revealing four hatches on top. It planes off for about half the total length of the vehicle, then drops around three feet. It levels off again over the engine compartment to the exhaust at the very rear. It lacks the distinct turret common to all tanks and is therefore a tracked vehicle. Equipped with a main winch mounted on the front above the spade, it is capable of wrenching up to 140 tons of dead weight. There is little if anything the M-88 cannot recover. Perhaps most impressive is the crane, or the "boom," as it is called. It extends from the front and passes the exhaust at the end. Normally, the crane is in the down position, flush with the top. One would never know it was a crane by simply glancing at it. Hydraulically operated, it is raised from pivot points next to my hatch and the driver's hatch in front. Powered by massive cylinders, it can lift up to thirty-five tons.

Hells Wrecker, and other M-88's like it, were the tow truck of the modern battlefield, and they cost the federal government two million dollars each. I later learned that an M-88-A2 Hercules from a neighboring unit was responsible for pulling down the statue of Saddam Hussein in Firdos Square of Baghdad, a small event in history with epic symbolism.

Hells Wrecker was a massive hulk with plenty of communications antennae sticking out the top. It looked important to enemy fighters, who might see it as a large, under-gunned communications vehicle—perhaps a command element in a long line of military vehicles. In order to fire the M2 .50 caliber machine gun at its top, the vehicle commander had to *get out* of his seat, standing in full view behind the trigger. It was effective with the right aim, but it required being fully exposed.

The rest of us were armed with the M-16 and M-9 Berettas, a few grenades, and four shoulder-fired AT-4 rocket launchers. But the enemy didn't know that. He would see an opportunity. All of us, the crew of three, had to pop out of our hatch to fire anything. It was dangerous to defend or attack in an M-88. Its crew typically had little training on how to respond to a threat from our seats. Though we were all riflemen by training, we were surprisingly unprepared for and exposed to an attack. The designers of the M-88-A2, United Defense & Anniston Army Depot, took little regard to the tactical effectiveness of Hells Wrecker, giving it a rather defenseless inch-thick steel armor penetrable by any caliber larger than 30 mm, and a single M2 .50 caliber on top. The M-88 was not supposed to be on the front lines. So, I suppose I was nervous.

If I was unprepared in Hells Wrecker, then the opposite was true of the tank crews that made up our company. They were professionals like I was, but they were the primary combat element in Bravo Company, whereas I was just an M-88 crewman and mechanic. With the turrets and firepower the M-88 lacked, the M1-A1 Abrams main battle tank was a sixty-eight-ton iron horse of mobile offensive combat power built by General Dynamics Land Systems. The 120 mm main gun projectiles could hit a target at 3,000 meters away. The blast of the cannon was so ferocious that it destabilized the tank, rocking it back and forth until the dust settled around it. Target practice was commonly done at a speed of 30 mph without reaching its maximum speed of 45 mph powered by a massive 1,500 hp jet turbine engine. Its armor was vastly superior to the Hells Wrecker, containing depleted uranium mesh-reinforced composite armor in the front end. It was capable of deflecting a direct hit from a 120 mm tank round harmlessly into the sky. The sleek angles were built to deflect large caliber rounds as long as the tank charged right at the enemy and as long as the enemy fired directly at its front.

In addition to forty rounds of main gun ammunition, there were nine hundred rounds for the M2 machine gun mounted on the commander's cupola, and about ten thousand rounds for the two M240 machine guns located on the loader's hatch and next to the main gun called the "coaxial." This most advanced tank in the world had cost the federal government about six million dollars. The Marines within were armed with M-9 Berettas, grenades, and a few rifles. In addition, each crew of four Marines were constantly training for battle. I would tell them that they had the best job in the world, whereas I, a mechanic, had the worst. Where they went to the range and blasted targets all day, I sometimes stayed up all night and fixed broken parts so they could do it all over again the following day. Tankers had all the fun and inevitably all the glory in combat, I told them, and they knew it. They also knew their success stood on a mechanic's shoulders.

The prospect of combat was slim for a mechanic, doomed to the shadows of war that are left out of textbooks, a line between a line. I had no idea what war was. None of my peers did. But that didn't stop history, and it didn't stop the Marines destined for Baghdad.

CHAPTER 11

Surviving Kuwait

A CLAP OF THUNDER echoed over my head; an ominous sky covered the Marines beginning a combat deployment. The rain tapped my face as I made my way to the commercial airline packed with troops. No sooner had I finished up my business than my feet were marching in step, weapon on shoulder, en route to Kuwait City.

The tanks were a few weeks ahead of us on ship with a skeleton crew of maintenance professionals to ensure their safe travel, but it was not the tanks I cared about, at least for the moment. Before my eyes was something I did not expect; through the rain, I watched wives seeing their husbands off with tears and pain I could only imagine from the outside looking in. I saw in their faces regret concerning things left undone or what could have been done to make their beloved husbands' journeys a little less difficult. In truth, these worries made the sorrow of it all the worse. The Marines themselves, not grasping the severity of their situation, gaped at their wives and girlfriends and children in wonder, and for some, it was at this point where they began to feel concern and re-evaluate what was coming for them. For the wives, this was what each had bargained for—the possibility of losing her husband to his country. I could only thank God that I didn't have a wife then, or girlfriend, for that matter; I would not be able to bear her up through the cheerless moment.

I was glad at the moment that none of those tears were for me. My attitude and determination were dead set, ready for what was to come. The sight of loved ones like weeping children would only cause me to second guess myself and my state of mind to falter. Thank God I didn't have children.

Heavy on my mind was the nature of war. Every war has its motives, but when men are sent to die for a cause, they should be sent without question that what they fight for is just and honorable. There remained mysteries, gaps in my train of thought where answers needed to be filled. I had the entire eighteen-hour flight to figure it out, and my mind was clearer, no doubt, than some of my comrades. So, behind us were our families, far below the clouds, and we had each other—like it or not—for the duration of the war.

All that I had done to prepare myself, the material and immaterial, culminated here. Those silent walks on favorite woodland trails to center myself, I yearned for them now. I knew that I would desire these things more than gold when I stepped foot off my homeland. All of this was anticipated—all except for the feelings that struck me hard in the chest concerning what I was marching off into. I began asking myself questions. *Why I am going to war outside my duty to wage war? Who stands to gain from forcing Saddam Hussein off his throne? And what is going to happen afterwards?* It became obvious to me that there were more moving parts to this invasion than met the eye.

Looking out the airline window, I listened to a brief history compiled by Marines for Marines, and from what I gathered, Saddam Hussein deserved what was coming for him. The history of his cruelty to the Iraqi and the Kurdish people was no small matter, and justice, according to our leadership, needed to be served. After the insertion of this idea, I immediately questioned, *Are we the ones who ought to serve it?* Our superiors made sure to inform us of his malice to satisfy our thirst for information, but it was plain that they had no real answer to this most pertinent question. We took this information gladly, however, and made it a justification for building forces to combat against him because, in truth, most of the enlisted men didn't care. Their minds were focused on a wife or girlfriend far away. Saddam Hussein was merely a job, an object. I later surmised that any personal anger a Marine directed toward the Iraqi dictator was because he believed Saddam to be the cause of all his misfortune—the gas chamber, anthrax shots, scorching in the desert, eating nasty rations, and drinking hot water out of a canteen. It might get bloody, which would be a bonus for most Marines, but however we whined, in the end we were all subject to the requirements of service.

★ ★ ★ ★ ★

As soon as the doors opened, the dry air leached the moisture from my body. I stepped off the airliner onto a seven-ton truck and began to sweat immediately. Welcome to Kuwait. It was eighty degrees in late January, and I was in full gear—a seventy-pound Alice pack, a new set of desert camouflage utilities, my weapons, helmet, load-bearing vest, flak jacket, gas mask and about twenty pounds of other stuff, including my journals, that I needed for deployment.

After a few minutes of driving we began to see civilians, Kuwaitis. I grabbed at my pistol, thinking they were going to jump in the truck and get me. If I could have put more distance between us, I would have. I had never seen an Arab before—that is, an Arab wearing a *shemagh* and *shora*, the unique headdress wound with a black rope and a flowing "man-skirt," as the Marines called it. There were only a few of them, and they posed no threat whatsoever to the entire battalion of Marines armed to the teeth, but I could not help looking at them with suspicion. We all did. It was a classic culture shock, and indeed, we must have frightened them seeing all of us staring. We very quickly developed a fatalistic attitude: If they had a bomb, they could take us out before we could react. It was the way we viewed all Arabs.

We didn't understand them, their language, their customs, or what they wore, so naturally we viewed them as an enemy. We spent the rest of the war keyed up around the Arabs, thinking their bullets and bombs could get us at any time, and there was little we could do about it. We were on guard around Kuwaitis as well, even though they were our allies, and we soon viewed Iraqis the same way. In my frustration at being around them, I began to write.

History: the victor's story. I have always loved a good story, and I knew in my heart this one would be written favoring the United States. Some excellent books have been written about Marines in Iraq, but not necessarily about 2nd Tank Battalion. A few of these include *Ambush Alley* by Tim Pritchard, *The March Up: Taking Baghdad with the U.S. Marines* by Bing West and Major General Ray L. Smith, *The Highway War: A Marine Company Commander in Iraq* by Major Seth B. Folsom, *Thunder Run: The Armored Strike to Capture Baghdad* by David Zucchino, *Heavy Metal: A Tank Company's Battle to Baghdad* by Captain Jason Conroy, *The Iraq War* by Williamson Murray and Major General Robert H. Scales Jr., and *Marines in the Garden of Eden: The True Story of Seven Bloody Days in Iraq* by Richard S. Lowry.

These are the best books about Marines in Iraq I have read, but even they contain just glimpses of what it was like to be a tanker, much less the context that makes history. It will be years before the public sees more released government documents on Operation Iraqi Freedom and a true picture of the invasion emerges. Historians digging into the "how" and "why" after the release of information make the history books. In other words, even though a myriad of books and articles have been published, they do not and cannot contain the full story of Iraq or of Operation Iraqi Freedom.

We will have to be content, for the moment, with what historians can glean from men who were there. The Marines. Everyday life at war. I was determined to tell the full story from the moment I began writing; posterity demanded it.

What we should have done in the First Gulf War was solve all of this before it began, and a decade before the US would have all the reason in the world to take Baghdad. Saddam's forces invaded Kuwait on August 2, 1990. The United Nations Security Council called on Saddam to withdraw his forces from Kuwait by January 15, 1991, or else face retaliation. Hussein's refusal to meet the deadline resulted in the conflict well known as Operation Desert Storm. Back then, Iraq had a motive, and that was to turn Kuwait into a province. Hussein noticed the potential benefits of such an invasion—specifically, oil. Kuwait's size made no difference compared to the value of what lay beneath its soil; cheap oil made it one of the most powerful countries on earth.

Saddam had a plan, but what was our plan? What did the United States of America stand to gain from a victory in the Middle East? To ease our conscience by doing something about terrorism? I pondered the reasons over and over again, with increasingly more possibilities than I could handle.

At the time, I was an angry twenty-year-old and I wrote extensively in my journal about how pissed off I was on being sent to Iraq when there were protests erupting all over the world. It didn't feel right, and my words reflected my anger:

> The intentions of America have changed from what I believe our founding fathers had intended. Taking into consideration the state at which our country was in during the Revolutionary War, our ambitions were pure. We believed in one idea, and that was to break free from the solid hold of Britain; nowhere in our minds was the idea of sending our forces afar. Keeping the tyrant from our lands was of utmost concern. In 1774, John Hancock made an interesting point addressing the need of a military:

> Since standing armies are so hurtful to a state, perhaps my countrymen may demand some substitute, some other means of rendering us secure against the incursions of a foreign enemy. But can you be one moment at a loss? Will not a well-disciplined militia afford ample security against foreign foes? From a well-regulated militia we have nothing to fear. Their interest is the same as that of the state. They do not jeopardize their lives for a master who considers them only as the instruments of his ambition, and whom they regard only as the daily dispenser of their scanty pittance of bread and water. No! They fight for their houses, their lands, for their wives, their children, for all who claim the tenderest names, and are held dearest in their hearts. They fight for their liberty, for themselves, and for their God.

My rant continued:

> To see the blueprint that the earliest Americans were creating is not difficult from this standpoint. They had foreseen if we had a military at our disposal, no matter what its intentions, those intentions could be used for personal benefit or profit. Thus America would turn into another Rome, or become another conquering wave of Vikings, killing and pillaging for wealth.

My journal is a window to a time when I was unsure of my leadership, from the platoon level to the president of the United States. I took the time to write an irregular poem about it, because no veteran discussed their experiences, commonly the Gulf War, or the tactics that would be of use to us. It produced a noticeable lack of combat proficiency later in the war because we were not able to apply the tactical lessons of the last war to ours. It was a mystery to me why no one talked about it, though we all knew about it, and I can only say it must have been deeply personal, the blood and the carnage, to mute them.

To my Leadership

Why didn't you tell me about your wars?
The bullets flying, the bombs and the wounded.
I could have gleaned something from you, but instead, I had to learn for myself
You are selfish
Keeping those secrets
When I could have been better for it.
What was it that you were keeping? What precious secrets I could have learned.
I still would have fought, contrary to what you think
No matter how awful a truth you revealed.

I voted for George W. Bush, and I was not, at the time, proud of it. I might have later blamed Saddam Hussein for my being in Iraq in the first place, but I, like everyone else, blamed the president too. Even among the military ranks, it was popular to blame President Bush for our current situation. But, like it or not, George W. Bush will go down in history for leading the United States through 9/11 and succeed in invading Iraq afterward.

The Bush Doctrine of going abroad to meet enemies before they could attack was not something I paid much attention to at the time, though I should have. I am cognizant now of my ignorance then of world affairs. I knew only the workings of my platoon and the tanks I had to care for. That aside, the Bush Doctrine was a monumental strategy that propelled the US military to the ends of the earth and expanded the influence of the United States across the globe. It was the Monroe Doctrine on crack; it gave the US military the right to unilaterally pursue any threat to the Unites States *outside* the Western Hemisphere. The National Security Strategy of the United States published on September 17, 2002, by the Bush Administration clearly states our strategy at the time:

> The security environment confronting the United States today is radically different from what we faced before. Yet the first duty of the United States Government remains what it always has been: to protect the American people and American interests. It is an enduring American principle that this duty obligates the government to anticipate and counter threats, using all elements of national power, before the threats can do grave damage. The greater the threat, the greater the risk of inaction—and the more compelling the case for taking anticipatory action to defend ourselves, even if uncertainty remains as to the time and place of the enemy's attack. There are few greater threats than a terrorist attack with WMD.
>
> To forestall or prevent such hostile acts by our adversaries, the United States will, if necessary, act preemptively in exercising our inherent right of self-defense. The United States will not resort to force in all cases to preempt emerging threats. Our preference is that nonmilitary actions succeed. And no country should ever use preemption as a pretext for aggression.[2]

---

[2] The Bush Doctrine, www.state.gov/documents/organization/63562.pdf

This was a natural action from an administration that had endured such a horrific attack as 9/11. I could not blame President Bush, though many did. On February 14, 2003, the United Nations Security Council reported that there were no weapons of mass destruction (WMDs) in Iraq. With this report, more than three million people protested in Rome the following day. It was the day the world rose up in one voice against the oncoming war, according to newspapers.[3] There were demonstrations in London and Barcelona of more than a million each. In San Francisco and New York, more than 200,000 protestors turned out, with more everywhere in between.[4] Fourteen million people across the globe participated in protest that day alone.[5] Protestors carried banners that said, *NOT IN OUR NAME!* and *THE WORLD SAYS NO TO WAR!* All the while, President Bush exacerbated the friction, saying, "We will go in [Iraq] with or without the approval of the UN."

At the time, I had only been in Kuwait for two weeks, and I was totally ignorant of how massive the protests were. News was slow coming in Kuwait, and when it arrived our leadership filtered it out. They did not want the Marines to think about the oncoming war. Independent thinking was discouraged. Most of us didn't care anyway. The tanks had just arrived, rolling off the carriers to our base, Life Support Area 5 (LSA-5), north of Kuwait City and twenty-five miles from the border of Iraq, with plenty to do besides. Personal mail hadn't arrived yet, and would not for two weeks, so for the time being we had no idea what was going on in the world. We had no idea what our wives and girlfriends were thinking, and that pissed us off. By the time mail arrived on February 13, we were desperate

---

3 Bennis, Phyllis, February 15, 2003. "The Day the World Said No to War," Institute for Policy Studies,
February 15, 2003, http://www.ips-dc.org/february_15_2003_the_day_the_world_said_no_to_war/
4 Tharoor, Ishaan, "Viewpoint: Why Was the Biggest Protest in World History Ignored?" Time Magazine, February 15, 2013. http://world.time.com/2013/02/15/viewpoint-why-was-the-biggest-protest-in-world-history-ignored/
5 Bennis.

for it, and the care packages that a few of us received were envied by all and shared by all.[6]

My interaction with the lower-ranking Marines was something the officers in our company wish they could have. While huddled in the driver's compartment in a tank repairing an electric line, I had the chance to speak with a lance corporal named Andrew Kelly. He was my height, 5'7", young, with a pointy nose and high cheekbones. I scarcely remember the conversation, or his first name, but my fellow mechanic received the ridicule of nearly all in our company, just because he was different.

Several Marines received a level of prejudice in Kuwait and Iraq, mostly because they were saved. He was a born-again Christian, and he refused to take part in many of the activities that the other Marines did, namely pornography, smoking, and crass behavior. The tank I was working on had carnal posters taped all through it, and I remember Kelly refusing to work on the tank because of it. Marines naturally took hold of this and made fun of him. They poked fun, I laughed it off, but Kelly was worse. An upstanding Marine was supposed to be the captain of the football team, supposed to have many flings at once, supposed to be a man's man, supposed to tell his secrets without being asked; Kelly was none of that. Misunderstood, he was quiet all the time, and I felt for him. Morale was low for him, as it was for many others I chanced to speak to, and these were mainly Marines of low rank who did most of the hard duties around camp, like pulling guard duty.

On the night of February 24, there was an event that showed me the true nature of morale in our company. One of the newer Marines to the company refused to stand guard duty. He mouthed off to a corporal just as I stepped in. I gave him a piece of my mind because I was obligated to enforce military discipline. His stubbornness was

---

6   There were no phones, no computers, no means but mail to communicate with the outside. Mail was slow in Kuwait. According to my journal, B Co received its first letters on February 13; not many but a few of us heard from home at this time.

getting in the way of his bearing, I told him. For his insubordination, he was doomed to stand guard duty the following day.

Stepping over a sand dune to his foxhole, I took the time to go and see him afterward. He was a lance corporal named Richard Johnson. In an even and fair manner, I asked him what was going on in his head to act like that. He told me he had no respect for the corporal he served under, that he was a hypocrite, that he was a liar. The lance corporal stood six and a half feet and was solid muscle; his eyes were bright and blue under the hot sun, pinpointed in anger. His strong chin went regularly unshaven like the rest of his face, but that did not matter. When I asked him about his feelings on the matter, his face turned red and his eyes began to wet. Through no action of mine, it was like I pulled a plug on a faucet. I knew there was something else.

"Is there something outside the Marine Corps that is bothering you?" I asked. He affirmed and tried to walk away as I touched his arm. "I am here if you want to talk," I offered, and he stalked away. He never again mentioned his problem, but he needed help. He needed a chaplain.

We rarely saw an actual chaplain in the field save at regimental functions, and even then he was mainly a figurehead offering prayer in front of all of us. There were only a handful of them for the entire armed services, 600 approximately, and they were all Navy officers trained as priests. It was difficult to get close to them as they were busy making Sunday rounds across Kuwait to the scattered division, each battalion separated by broad expanses of desert. Chaplains also tended to hover close to the command element, being officers, and by consequence it became difficult not to associate them with authority. Rarely did the priest visit a foxhole in which the lowest ranking held vigil, and when he did come by and visit a platoon, it was impossible to get close to him as the very request to do so was considered a weakness. If a Marine with a concern—even a minor one—wanted to see a chaplain for guidance, he had to ask permission from his corporal, who had to ask his sergeant, who asked a lieutenant, just to receive an audience. It *was* proper use of the chain of command, where everyday issues could be solved before they reached the ears of an officer, but when a Marine had a *private* issue to deal with, it became a subject of anxiety for everyone.

No one usually knew what was going on, but they all knew *something* was going on because the Marine was duty-bound to use the chain of command to solve his problem. It might be a sick grandmother back home that worried him, or a fellow Marine he wanted to strangle. But no matter what the crisis, everyone of authority came to know of it, and gossip funneled it to everyone else. For weeks afterward, the Marine would find himself besieged by suspicion as if he were subversive in some way for asking an audience with a priest.

The arousal of curiosity was one factor, but I began to believe that the element of instability it represented to the rest of the Marines worried them most. They were engaged in a tactical situation, and a Marine with secrets represented a mental side of the situation they didn't get, understanding only that it *was* a factor of concern. Everyone had a right to be worried, and most by consequence kept their secrets to themselves. Chaplains commonly moved on without knowing a platoon's morale was in the toilet, abuses in power were rank, or a Marine might desperately need attention.

The absence of a chaplain's guidance to the low-ranking and destitute produced, however, the most remarkable men on the front, who became beacons of light to those in need. The layperson was the gateway to God in the minds of many a Marine. The "lay reader" was an unofficial title which garnered no special honors to those who held it yet sometimes was absolutely essential to the morale of the troop. Becoming one was easy. The Marine who desired the position simply had to ask a superior, and it was granted him if he had a Bible and wished to use it for the benefit of others. It was with him always, on and off duty, and on occasion he led his peers in prayer when he saw fit or when requested of him.

A good lay reader took every opportunity to spread the gospel and pray. Mostly, though, since some Marines didn't like to be preached to, the recourse was prayer. Everyone understood it and needed it. Even those who were not Christian, which was many. Lay readers were perhaps more important than the commissioned chaplains because they were in the dust like everyone else; they shot rifles, dug the foxholes, pulled the duty, and were as sand-soaked as everyone else. They were also *not* officers, and that was essential to their popularity among the enlisted. That thought inspired me to write this poem.

The Desert of Abraham

It was the desert of Abraham, and few of us knew it.
Few of us were true Christians, though all of us called ourselves Christians
   We knew sand, the relentless heat, warped metal, and a trigger.
   So when you saw Christians you knew it, they knew of Abraham, they carried a Bible, and somehow they were a gateway for the rest of us heathens to glimpse God.
   When, all we had to do is pray.

★ ★ ★ ★ ★

The tank maintenance crew had big problems to deal with. "The flow of replacement parts while in Kuwait was a 0% fill rate," according to the Bravo Company after action report.[7] We despaired at not being better prepared to repair the tanks as they needed it, but to be honest it was not our fault. I understood that there was a myriad of responsibilities our generals had to deal with in preparing for an invasion, but they totally neglected tank maintenance. We were able to patch and repair parts based on our own ingenuity, and with what little we brought with us from the States. I distinctly

---

7   B Co After Action Report. "Logistics Discussion."

remember ripping apart a cardboard box found in our rations to make a gasket for a hydraulic turret servo that was spraying fire-resistant hydraulic fluid all over the tank driver. Other times, we banged out air filters filled with sand, and sprayed out fuel filters clogged with impurities, and used improper oils to lubricate engines. Our captain lauded us for accomplishing an "incredible operation" with such limited means, and he was right.[8] Therefore, by the time we reached Baghdad, most tanks were combat capable, but far from mission capable.[9]

In the tankers' minds, I was the one they wanted on their tanks. Even if I didn't know how to fix something, my presence was infinitely favored over other mechanics, and they were patient with me as I tried to figure something out. They frequently said that they didn't worry about me on their tanks as I would not "walk off" with anything. I was trustworthy, and that, according to any tanker, was gold.

Gear still frequently went missing, causing the tankers to always be on guard. Since it was the mechanics' prerogative to fix the tanks, they ultimately had the say on which parts were necessary for what tank and what parts weren't. So, when a mechanic was working on a tank, a tanker was assigned to "keep him company" while he worked, talking as normal, but we all knew that he was there to make sure the mechanics were honest.

It was hard to blame the mechanic for stripping good parts off a perfectly good tank to fix another, as sometimes happened. Parts were so deficient in Kuwait and Iraq that it was necessary in order to keep the tanks moving. The orders came from the top, and what was the lowly mechanic to do except follow them? For some reason, I was spared from the dreadful order that pissed off tankers, and never had to violate a working tank, but during the war, when we spotted a down M1-A1 that had been hit by enemy fire or was designated

---

8   Ibid.
9   Gordon, John, and Bruce Pirnie, "Everybody Wanted Tanks." JFQ issue 39.

as a "parts tank," we pulled no punches. It was survival. We hurried with our wrenches to strip the tank for parts, and before long all that remained was a hull full of holes and dripping hydraulic lines, removed cables and dissected control panels. At the end of the war, these unfortunate beasts were lined up in Kuwait where any passerby could see the full necessity of survival during the war; the tanks with every conceivable missing part, track missing, sprockets gone, and depleted uranium armor snatched, hatches hanging open for all to pillage what was inside.

Outside robbing Peter to pay Paul, there was the waiting. The few books I brought with me from home had circulated among the company so much that the covers were ripped off, spines all but gone, wrapped up and held together by rubber bands. Still, the Marines continued to read. A few of the favorites that I had brought were *Dune* by Frank Herbert, *The Ten Thousand* by Michael Curtis Ford, and *Hamlet* by Shakespeare, all completely unsalvageable by the war's end. The waiting caused our minds to wander and morale to drop. After I read my books, my journal received the most illuminating thought—that I actually found myself falling in love with the desert, even if I was not there by choice:

> Here in the desert of Kuwait, sands brush my face each day just as the previous one. One thing I can say is that these sands give way to thought ... too much thought at times. The peaceful desolation of this place astounds me, clearing my head of all that is trivial. This world is completely opposite of what I have lived in, and forces me to realize what an exulted life I had in the States. I arrived in Kuwait about a month ago ... when camp was silent, and without knowing how long I would remain. As a simple Marine, my life is leveled on the basis of order. Simple as it should be: go and kill the enemy.

Men once tried to reach God in this land I am about to invade. They called it the Tower of Babel. The Lawgiver Hammurabi and his capital at Babylon sat close to Baghdad. The Hanging Gardens stood here once too. This is the land of Gilgamesh, a legend to the Iraqi people; a great story of a God-created man and his quest to become immortal. I also am about to conquer this Mesopotamia now as Sargon the Great once did. Like the Assyrians, the Chaldeans, the Greeks, the Persians, the Romans, the Ottoman Turks, and the British once did. These sands become a story before me, instead of the simplicity of dust. I see in the earth destroyed stone battlements. Houses are enveloped in trash, and charred from fire. Half buried dreams scatter this land that once belonged to smiling faces . . . now the land solely possesses the sadness that followed them. I frown at the thought that I may be next in this dark string of history. Only, I believe, affecting those uninvolved; to scar their dreams like these charred homes once filled with laughter. All of this for the sole motive of fulfilling and bringing to light the dreams of another. Am I unlike the crusaders of long ago? Or do I simply follow the officers who command me? I believe soldiers throughout time have gone through this same moral battle as I.[10]

My thoughts often drifted to Saddam Hussein. On or about February 18, he survived an assassination attempt by one of his bodyguards. The failed attempt made us all hope that there was still a diplomatic solution to war. But common sense dictated that

---

10   Grant, Aaron. "Journal of Corporal Aaron M. Grant." September 11, 2001–March 21, 2003. P 138, entry February 28, 2003.

regardless of what happened to Saddam we were going to invade anyway; we didn't come halfway across the world to just go home again. Saddam knew that. But there was much he didn't know, made possible because of the atmosphere of fear he created in his regime. He was absolutely sure the fighting prowess of his military would stop any assault the Americans could muster. Americans did not win wars anymore. Americans would lose their nerve just like they did in Vietnam. It was logical, but not probable. Life in the regime was a life of fear; understanding that Iraq was crippled by it sheds light on how Saddam could think this way.

Saddam Hussein maintained power by wanton murder since he and the Ba'ath Party took power in 1979. He immediately identified political rivals and executed sixty-six Ba'ath party leaders, replacing them with sycophantic "yes-men." He even video-taped the proceedings. Eight months later he attacked Iran with his army of 190,000 souls and 2,200 heavy tanks, stepping off the Iran-Iraq War that lasted until 1988.[11] While the bloody war played out, eventually causing hundreds of thousands of deaths, he created a police state watching over civilians *and* the military that rivaled the Kremlin in the Soviet Union. Everyone was afraid. Any dissenters—any with opinions that differed from Ba'athism, any who plotted against the regime, and *any who expressed independent thought*—conveniently disappeared. An atmosphere of fear permeated Iraq. Saddam was well known to personally execute subversives and order assassinations, torture by acid-baths, and sentence dissenters to the basement of the Olympic Committee headquarters where a nail-lined sarcophagus awaited the unfortunate person.[12] Over the course of his twenty-four-year reign of terror, it is estimated that Saddam killed a million people in war and peace and incarcerated even more. One of his favorite

---

11 "Iran-Iraq War (1980-1988)" GlobalSecurity.org, accessed August 18, 2015, http://www.globalsecurity.org/military/world/war/iran-iraq.htm
12 Burns, John, "Soccer Players Describe Torture by Saddam's Son," The New York Times, May 6, 2003, http://www.nytimes.com/2003/05/06/international/worldspecial/06TORT.html

Stalinist maxims was "If there is a person, then there is a problem. If there is no person, then there is no problem."[13]

Putting aside his wanton practices, Saddam by all accounts was a colorful man with a shred of brilliance. He created a popular romance novel, *Zabiba and the King*, published in 2000. He tried to stay anonymous, but it didn't last. The regional best seller quickly turned into a full-blown musical. From 1968 to 1979, he created a national literacy program where if an Iraqi didn't attend, he would be thrown in jail. UNESCO even honored him for eliminating illiteracy in Iraq. He was by all accounts a prolific builder, creating hospitals, schools, and roads in Iraq, yet he destroyed an entire civilization in his own borders. The Marsh Arabs of the south were eliminated in the Iran-Iraq War because he believed they sided with the enemy. He drained the 9,000-square-kilometer marsh to a mere remnant by the time the Marines arrived in 2003. During the 1991 invasion of Kuwait, he was surprised to hear that President Bush Sr. condemned the Iraqi invasion. Based on a conversation with US Ambassador April Galespie, Saddam thought the US couldn't care less about "Arab-Arab" conflicts. The Iraqi troops didn't expect US intervention at all, especially since their dictator was so "friendly" to America.

Years before, he tried to give America ninety-four million dollars to lift the "homeless and wretched Americans living in poverty." Though the effort never materialized, he made friends in America. He was honored with the key to the city of Detroit after he donated a large sum of money to a Chaldean Christian church in the city. Sanctioned by Mayor Coleman Young, the reverend of the church visited Saddam in Iraq where the public exchange was made. Saddam had a flair for diplomacy. In order to dodge a war with the US, the dictator offered to debate President Bush on live television. Of course, the president didn't oblige, but it demonstrated his willingness to be forthright with the issues. He pleaded with no response.

---

13   Burns, John, "The World; How Many People Has Hussein Killed?" *The New York Times*, Jan 26, 2003, http://www.nytimes.com/2003/01/26/weekinreview/the-world-how-many-people-has-hussein-killed.html

"This is something proposed in earnest out of my respect for the people of the United States, the people of Iraq, and the people of the world. I call for this because war is not a joke." Ebbing into insanity, he even had a Qur'an made that was written in *his own blood*. The sacrilege of the act didn't stop him. Over the course of a decade he gave *fifty pints* of blood for the project, written by a well-known calligrapher. Where the Blood Qur'an is today is a mystery.

Most Marines did not know the history of how Saddam came to power, and how the United States made that history. In the late 1950s, the CIA was interested in stopping the spread of communism in Iraq, which was being seeded throughout the country by General Abdul Qassem, a member of the Iraqi Ministry of Defense. The CIA allied itself to the anti-communist Ba'athist Party in which Saddam was a twenty-two-year-old aspiring member. The CIA orchestrated an assassination plot to kill the general with Saddam playing a leading role. The assassination failed when Saddam pulled the trigger too soon.[14] The young Saddam fled, with the assistance of the CIA, to a tiny foxhole in his hometown, Tikrit—the same foxhole where US forces found him hiding in December 2003. From there he fled to Cairo, where he assumed close ties to the American embassy there.[15] Saddam later took power in 1979, and he would have the backing of the United States again in the war with Iran he initiated six months later.

In 1982, President Ronald Reagan supported Iraq, stating that America could not allow Iraq to lose its southern oil fields to the Iranian Shia militants. He gave billions in military supplies and loans

---

14   Sale, Richard, "Saddam Key in Early CIA Plot," *United Press International*, April 10, 2003, http://www.globalpolicy.org/security/issues/iraq/history/2003/0410saddam.htm
15   Morris, Roger, "A Tyrant 40 Years in the Making," *The New York Times*, March 14, 2003, http://query.nytimes.com/gst/fullpage.html?res=9505EFDB103E F937A25750C0A9659C8B63&scp=1&sq=saddam%20morris&st=cse

to the regime.[16] With the weapons and money came supplies for making chemical weapons and derivatives of chemical agents that were later put together in Iraq and used on the Iranians.[17] The US gave Saddam Hussein chemical weapons. In 1986, the United States Department of Commerce licensed seventy biological agents to Iraq, including at least twenty-one shipments of anthrax,[18] a decision the US would soon regret in the Gulf War, where Saddam used chemical weapons against the American military.[19] Saddam used mustard gas on the Kurds who had rebelled in northern Iraq in 1988, and it was after this incident that the US policy toward Iraq began to change, especially when Saddam invaded Kuwait in August 1990.

Had most Marines known the true reason we all wore gas masks and got anthrax shots, they would have viewed the oncoming war differently. The chemical weapons President Bush demanded, the WMD, was given to Iraq by the US.[20] To be fair, it was a United States of a different time, and a different administration with different goals. We were, however, more concerned with the Iraqi military at the time than we were with history.

★ ★ ★ ★ ★

Saddam's military was paralyzed with fear. The Republican Guard was created to watch over the regular army, where the ideology of

---

16   The CIA played one side against the other the entire war. If it wasn't funding Iraq, then it was funding Iran in some way because the US government feared both Iran's Ayatollah Khomeini, and the socialist Saddam Hussein.
17   Schaller, Michael, *Reckoning with Raegan: America and its President in the 1980s*, New York: Oxford University Press, 1992, 139-40.
18   King, John, *Arming Iraq: A Chronology of U.S. Involvement*, History of Iran, March 2003, accessed September 7, 2015, http://www.iranchamber.com/history/articles/arming_iraq.php
19   The Gulf War Syndrome is proof that chemical weapons were used against the American military in 1991. The chemical weapons Saddam had were usually destroyed by American forces rather than used by Iraqi forces; but the residual effects of the detonation nevertheless had an effect on American troops.
20   Milhollin, Gary, "Licensing Mass Destruction: U.S. Exports to Iraq: 1985-1990," Wisconsin Project on Nuclear Arms Control, June 1991, http://www.wisconsinproject.org/countries/iraq/LicenseMD.html

the party trumped patriotism to country.[21] The Special Republican Guard, screened for loyalty, had privileges no others had, occupying and defending Baghdad and thwarting any attacks on Saddam's regime. The Fedayeen Saddam and the Ba'ath militia, his most loyal fanatics, were embedded in all units as well to ensure loyalty and to execute those who did not fight.[22] They were all controlled by the Special Security Organization, which had spies throughout the ranks to ensure loyalty. To make matters worse for the military, the separate branches were forbidden to contact one another. In order to ensure his prominence, and to ensure that the military could not rise up and remove him from power, Saddam forbade inter-branch contact even for security reasons.

The result was that Iraqi military units—from regulars to militia— didn't know what one another was doing. In order to discover who was on the flanks, each branch had to send out reconnaissance and visually and verbally make contact with sister branches. For example, if the regular army was making maneuvers around the capital Baghdad, the Special Republican Guard, who were stationed in Baghdad, had to send out scouts and report back what they found. Only Saddam and his sons knew the locations of all forces. A commander of the Special Republican Guard wrote, "I had no relation with any other units or fighting forces. No other units were allowed near our unit. No visits between officers [of the different military organizations] were ever allowed."[23]

All operations, therefore, were clandestine. General was forbidden to associate with general for fear of Saddam, and Saddam feared their corroboration for fear of a coup d'état. A culture of lies fed the regime. Everyone lied to appease Saddam because he punished, imprisoned,

---

21 Kevin Woods, Michael Pease, Mark Stout, Williamson Murray, and James Lacey, "The Iraqi Perspectives Project: A View of Operation Iraqi Freedom from Saddam's Senior Leadership," The Joint Center for Operational Analysis, vii.
22 "Saddam Executes 60 Iraqi Officers," *The Scotsman*, March 27, 2003, http://www.scotsman.com/news/world/saddam-executes-60-iraqi-officers-1-601169
23 Iraqi Perspectives Project interview of Barzan Abd Al-Ghafur Sulayman Al-Tikriti, Commander, Special Republican Guard, 16 November 2003.

and murdered anyone who gave him bad news. Officers recalled how a brigadier general was imprisoned for a year for bringing bad news to the dictator.[24] They were also well aware that some officers disappeared after angering Saddam with the truth.[25] For example, in 1994 Saddam executed three field officers and purged a dozen more for telling the truth about his son Uday Hussein.[26] After the Gulf War in 1991, bad news was rife, especially when it concerned the military, and Saddam wanted none of it. Iraqi lieutenant general Raad Hamdani said, "It was around this time, 1996 and 1997, that everyone started lying. Everyone started lying a lot. They lied about things like 'we won the 1991 war' and such as that."[27]

When one of Iraq's best generals suggested that the Iraqi military was lagging, Saddam berated him in front of his peers, saying his analysis provided no referents.[28] In fear for their lives, in fear for their families, everyone touted the excellence of the Iraqi military and the excellence of their commander in chief. Telling the truth simply was not to one's benefit. Lying kept one alive; lying put food on the table. From the lowest ranking officer to the highest, they paid homage in words in order to keep Saddam happy. The true state of the Iraqi military was no secret to everyone else, well kept from Saddam, and in deplorable condition.[29]

One Iraqi general later stated that the Iraqi Army "had been

---

24 Kevin Woods, Michael Pease, Mark Stout, Williamson Murray, James Lacey, "Iraqi Perspectives Project: A View of Operation Iraqi Freedom from Saddam's Senior Leadership," The Joint Center for Operational Analysis, 8.
25 Makiya, Kanan. *Republic of Fear: The Politics of Modern Iraq*. Los Angeles: University of California Press, 1998. 292-296.
26 "Saddam Executes 60 Iraqi Officers," *The Scotsman*, March 27, 2003. Accessed August 21, 2015.
27 Recollections of General Raad Hamdani in "Perspectives II Republican Guard Corps," from Woods, *A View*, 9.
28 Ibidem.
29 I owe the entirety of this paragraph to the research of the team at the Joint Center for Operational Analysis. Thanks to their efforts, the regime can be studied where it was normally closed to foreigners.

systematically destroyed over time as no other army in history."[30] He was right. By 1990, it was the fourth largest army in the world, numbering over a million men, and contained, among thousands of other troop carriers, 5,500 to 6,700 main battle tanks (T-55, T-62, and T-72), mainly purchased from the Soviet Union.[31] The 1991 Gulf War changed all that. After being soundly defeated, it retained about a third of the manpower and tanks it had before the war.[32] Economic sanctions after the Gulf crippled the Iraqi Army as well. It was nearly impossible to supply and repair the damaged tanks, not only because Iraq lacked its own production facilities, but also because the United Nations imposed a financial and trade embargo after the Gulf War that severely hampered Iraq's ability to resupply its rolling stock.[33] One estimate states that as much as 50 percent of Iraq's rolling stock was deficient of necessary parts.[34] However, the Iraqi army was able to furnish supplies from the black market and keep up a healthy arsenal of small arms all the while.

Not only had American forces been massing in Kuwait since January, they had also been bombing southern Iraqi air defenses since before the official start of the war. It began in the Clinton administration as Operation Desert Fox in 1998, reoccurred most recently in June 2002, and intensified in the weeks before the invasion. Four thousand strike and support "sorties" in Iraq's no-fly zones were made from the first to the twentieth of March alone.[35]

The US deployed 83,906 Marines along the Kuwait/Iraq border and elsewhere, along with 340,092 of every other branch of the armed services deployed throughout Iraq's borderlands and sea. Our

---

30   General Qahtan al-Tamimi, May Ying Welsh, "U.S. Trains Proxy to Quell resistance," Aljazeera.net, June 6 2004, http://english.aljazeera.net/NR/excres/554FAF3A-B267-427A-BQEC-54881BDEOA2E.ht (as of June 10, 2004).
31   Cordesman, *The Military Balance*, 302-303.
32   Ibidem.
33   Cordesman, *The Military Balance*, 293.
34   *Jane's Defense Weekly*, February 5, 2003, http://www4.janes.com/K2/doc-print.jsp?K2DocKey=/content1/janesdata/mags/jdw/history
35   Hosmer, *Iraqi Resistance*, 75.

British allies deployed 40,906 with a small force of 2,050 Australians, 194 Polish troops, and 31 Canadians, totaling a multinational force 467,177 strong.[36] A portion of this, the most advanced coalition in the world, faced the Iraqi 6th and 10th armored divisions stationed in southern Iraq, along with the 51st Mechanized Division supported by the 11th, 14th, and 18th infantry divisions[37]—a conservative total of 500 aged tanks and 32,000 troops against the American force of approximately 330 modern tanks and 60,000 souls.[38] And they were just north of us, right over the border. Assuming we faced a motivated force of Iraqi soldiers, potentially the greatest fight of the war was imminent.

Hindsight is a beautiful thing. In hindsight, I should have prayed that Saddam would not attack us in Kuwait. If he had, he would have caught us totally unprepared. Most of our munitions were not distributed until well after we arrived. What little we had was given to us in the States and limited to ammunition for our service weapons. So, there were no rockets, no grenades, and no main tank rounds, no mortars and no artillery to call on. All we had was the oversight of the Air Force for the first few weeks in Kuwait. If the Iraqis had attacked us, they would have received a tremendous fight for a few minutes of small arms fire, and then, exhausted, we would have charged with our unsharpened bayonets. They should have attacked us; why they didn't remained to me a mystery at the time. Researching the nature of the regime after the fact, it was obvious to me that no officer would have dared take the initiative to invade Kuwait just to get at us. Initiative was discouraged in the regime. Saddam did not like free-thinkers. Indeed, he was threatened by them and took steps to dispose of them.

---

36   Lt Gen. Moseley, Michael, "Operation Iraqi Freedom – by the Numbers: Assessment and Analysis Division," The United States Air Force, April 30, 2003, 3.
37   Col. Fontenot, Lt Col. Degen, and Lt Col. Tohn, "On point, Fort Leavenworth, Kansas: Combat Studies Institute Press," 2004, pp. 100-101, and "CFLCC Intelligence Update," March 23, 2003, 0300Z. "51st Mechanized Division," accessed August 9, 2012, http://www.globalsecurity.org/military/world/iraq/51mech.htm.
38   Ibidem.

★ ★ ★ ★ ★

One crisp morning in Kuwait, our captain made us don gas masks and run the perimeter of LSA-5. Running in the sand is difficult enough in a normal situation, but our captain aimed to make us superhuman. So, while sucking oxygen through our filter hole an inch wide, we kicked up a sandstorm that pissed off all the other Marines stationed at LSA-5 into the camp. It was laughable, but soon we were the sorry ones. Our sweat stuck to the seal between the masks and our faces, and we could not bat our eyes without salt seeping in them. Marines dropped like flies, hunching over or ripping their masks off to get more air. Most of us put a finger in the seal of the mask just to survive the run. Our leader at the front kept up his pace all the while, without cheating like the rest of us were. If one could see past the universal suffering of the company, one could perhaps be motivated by the sight of the captain leading his men.

On March 4, in order to keep us on our toes, someone high in the chain of command decided to stage a mock gas attack at LSA-5. We were playing cards or enjoying midday naps when suddenly I heard everyone shouting. I stood and a Marine looked at me and shouted, "GAS! GAS! GAS!" It normally took me nine seconds to remove the gas mask from my hip and have it on and functioning, but this time my nerves took hold. I fumbled with the head straps, and it took me twice as long to begin breathing filtered air. I ran around our neatly staged tanks and repeated the call as loud as I could through the hot mask. Everyone spread the word and within minutes we all were sucking air. We ran to the tents and got accountability, and we waited, unsure of what to do. Was this real? Nobody in the lower ranks knew.

For nearly an hour we lay on our sleeping bags sucking air. Most quickly fell asleep in their own sweat. I lay awake with nerves high, wondering if Saddam had attacked. When the order came to remove masks, we peeled the rubber from our faces with relief. I later wrote that "the silent killer brought me closer to mortality." It was not to be the last drill at LSA-5.[39]

★ ★ ★ ★ ★

On March 8, Captain Gunn mustered the company to view a crude terrain model of our plan to attack the southern and northern Rumaila oil fields, called "Opening Gambit."[40] The map in the sand helped us build situational awareness. After securing the oil fields intact, our key objective was to capture a massive bridge over the Saddam Canal. This didn't make sense to me. The bridge was sturdy enough to let tanks pass over and was the only one like it in the area. I raised my hand immediately.

"Sir, once we secure the bridge, are we going to destroy it?"

Everyone laughed. They were not thinking like I was. Like us, Saddam knew the value of that bridge to the US, so I assumed that Saddam would have the bridge destroyed to prevent us from crossing to engage his army. That would make the US divert to the west and up north to another bridge bypassing the most direct route to Baghdad. Additionally, a great part of Saddam's forces were positioned north of the bridge, and if we had chosen to destroy it, it would have bottled up the enemy tanks and troop carriers positioned there so they could not attack us if we were heading west. But this was not the plan. Instead, we were to go straight across the bridge, engaging the enemy and therefore opening a road to Baghdad. That was what everyone else was thinking, but they were not thinking strategically. Saddam would destroy it. Days later I had a chance to bring up my concern to the captain in person, remembering Patton's words: "If everyone is thinking alike, then somebody is not thinking."

★ ★ ★ ★ ★

---

39   Grant, *Journal*, 143.
40   Colonel Dunford, J.F., and J.L. Gibson, "Regimental Combat Team 5 Narrative Summary," 5th Marines, 1st Marine Division, 2003. 1.

Standing in the desert shaving one morning, I winced at the touch of my razor in the dry breeze. The purpose of shaving cream was a mystery at LSA-5. Immediately upon application, the climate sucked whatever moisture the foam once had into oblivion. The result was a glue-like residue nearly impossible to work out of the blade. Light sand blew my way, encrusting the already dry foam, creating facial sandpaper. Frustrated, I nearly pitched the razor out into the darkness. The morning stars crept to the orange glow of sunrise. I loved desert mornings. Chilly, dew on our tents, it was the opposite of the day that punished us with blistering sun.

After months of similar mornings, I grew fond of the emptiness—the complete absence of all that I had been brought up to see; the worries of a chaotic world dissolved into a cold chill. In the desert, the heart of nature beats close by. Men, grappling with it at first, are then captivated by its simplicity. Like swimming in warm waters, a vague memory hinted at the heart as our bodies become enveloped, no different from the sand. Earthly concerns faded in my mind; the splendor that remained was all the faith and dreams that a free mind could fathom. *Peace.*

Sifting the particles from my face, footsteps ground in the earth behind me. Turning, to my surprise Captain Gunn placed his shaving cup down nearby.

"How are you doing, Corporal Grant?" he asked.

"Fine, sir; attempting to shave." There was a long pause.

"So, what do you think of all of this?" he questioned.

"About our plan of attack, sir?"

"Sure."

I hesitated, thinking about how candid I should be.

"I think that the Rumaila Bridge will be destroyed before we get there," I said. The captain raised his eyebrows with a questioning glance.

"What makes you think that?"

"That's what I would do if I were in his shoes, sir."

He began to brush his teeth, grunting at my statement. He spat onto the ground.

"The command seems to think it's the best plan for our company now. They probably have thought of this the same as you."

He continued brushing as I splashed canteen water on my face. I looked in his direction and spoke.

"As far as being in the desert, sir, I cannot think of anywhere else I would rather be; but I cannot see the logic in this move."

"Hmmm." He started to speak but found no words. I gazed to the brightening sky in the east.

"The command believes it for the best, and we have to at least try."

"Yes sir," I said.

"They have the best minds on this now; that makes me feel comfortable." Hocking a mouthful, he spat once more. Zipping up my bag of gear, I stood, slightly taller than him.

"I'm off, sir. Good morning."

"I'll talk to you later, Grant," he returned. I stepped off back to the tents thinking about what faith the captain had in our leadership—an admirable trait. He was a man to whom none could be preferred during the time of war, I instantly realized. Bravo Company must trust this man wholeheartedly to the ends of the globe.

It was about this time that I noticed someone had scratched *apricot* into the side of one of our tanks. This would not be alarming to anyone but a tanker. Tankers are by nature superstitious, and the scratched taboo was taken seriously by many in Bravo. Legend had it that during WWII an entire tank battalion was eliminated by the Nazis and the only thing left untouched in the field of burning tanks, oddly, was the apricot rations the men had brought along with them. Since that time, tankers have had what I thought to be a silly idea that if a tank came anywhere near the word or apricots themselves it would be doomed to break down or be susceptible to some other unwanted catastrophe. Since we all were destined to go to Baghdad, we took such offenses seriously.

There were Marines that would not allow anyone near their tank who had eaten the fruit within twenty-four hours, and if Hawaiian Punch, which contained apricot juice, was found, or found to have been consumed by a crewman, Marines would call on a chaplain to bless the tank in order for the mission to continue. It was that serious.

Everyone searched about for the culprit, though no one came forward, so it was surmised that another company was at fault, and we reciprocated appropriately, scratching the word in their tanks without proof. At the time it didn't bother me. I had a full jar of apricot jelly in my rucksack on the M-88 that I received in a care package from back home. However, I didn't go around saying it as I knew guys had been beaten up over less. I kept quiet about it and enjoyed jelly on my meals in secret; I loved apricots in any form. I was not about to give up one of the few comforts I had in the desert. Apricots. I shook my head and cracked a smile. *How ridiculous*, I thought, watching tankers go nuts over the offense. I could never have guessed that my attitude toward the harmless fruit would *completely* change by the end of the war to come.

On March 9, the corporals were made to stand guard duty like the rest of the troops—those ranking lance corporal and below.[41] A corporal of the guard (COG) was caught sleeping on his twenty-four-hour duty post, so we all were put on the guard roster as a consequence. It had a massive impact on the morale of the NCOs of Bravo Company. *It made us look like idiots,* I wrote later in my journal, *because it undermined our authority with the troops.* Removing us from our responsibilities effectively put us on a level playing field as the troops. In other words, our leadership viewed us contemptuously. Our rank had little to no meaning to them, and the troops took full advantage of it. One of my lance corporals chose to mouth off to me afterward when he pleased; he even stole some of my gear, and there was no authority I could punish him with since us corporals were just like the troops now. My morale sank; I began

---

41   Grant, *Journal*, 144.

to hate Kuwait for being stuck there. My respect for the sergeants and officers waned, and all I could think of was my silent walks in the woods back home. It began to feel as if we would never leave Kuwait.

★ ★ ★ ★ ★

Military discipline relaxed week after week in Kuwait. Soon, I was the only Marine to show up to formation with all my combat gear. Marines bitched, fought one another, and became skinny and bored in LSA-5. They wore their green skivvy-shirts and desert camo bottoms and strutted around like John Wayne. In their boredom, they ran out of cigarettes, so they began to smoke tea leaves from tea bags found in our rations; the aroma, I was told, smelled just like pot. They fashioned bongs out of spare wood lying around and smoked whatever they could in that as well.[42] I was fortunate; I smoked like the rest of them, but I smoked a pipe. I had the foresight to bring a massive amount of loose-leaf tobacco, so I never ran out. By the time the Marines invaded Iraq, nobody except me had tobacco, and that affected morale. There were some who made it to the rear to get more at Camp Doha near Kuwait City. But they hoarded their cigarettes and sold them at a premium price to the rest of us who were stuck at LSA-5. Most bitched and bought them anyway.

I could not get Marines in my squad to wear their uniforms properly, and this was directly affected by their boredom around camp and the lack of authority the corporals now had. Everyone had gotten too comfortable, and unless you had a strong sergeant who committed to military discipline, the Marines turned into an undisciplined mob. Discipline came from the sergeant, and it was his responsibility to make sure we were ready for combat.

My platoon had a particularly weak sergeant, so we, by nature, became weak as well. I did what I could, but I was numbed by the lackadaisical atmosphere and soon believed that the troops didn't

---

42   I have a picture of my sergeant smoking a wooden bong he whittled as everyone laughed standing by.

respect me. After all, I was only one stripe higher than most of them. I found my motivation sagging; it was all I could do to keep up with my journal. I tired with reading, and I found myself often staring off into the desert blankly. Soon, for all the Marines stationed at LSA-5 there was nothing left but patience. We had to wait for the word to move the company, and that killed discipline. We waited in Kuwait for nearly sixty days.

Things heated up when we moved to our dispersal area approximately six miles from the Iraqi border on March 18. President Bush had set a deadline for Iraq to come clean with their WMD by the seventeenth or else face retaliation regardless of UN protests. That date passed, and we all anticipated the next move, which was to invade. The entire company had moved, which immediately strengthened morale. Finally, we were doing what we came to the Middle East to do. I had spent the last few days installing modifications on the tanks that would enable us to advance at night. All lights were to be turned off, and we were to rely upon night vision technology to follow the tanks into Iraq. We placed cardboard over the lights just to be sure no one used them. We placed infrared blinkers on every vehicle that could be seen by us but not Saddam's army unless they possessed infrared technology, which they did not. We also put infrared reflector panels on the tanks that were large enough to be seen miles away and from the air so we could identify ourselves to allies.

Each tank was also wired with its own personal GPS so the top brass could track our movements individually. Testing them at night was a spectacle indeed. I shut the hatch in the M-88 and looked through my infrared sight and saw a sea of flickering green bulbs, like fireflies, I imagined, back at home. Looking out the periscope without the night vision, one saw ominous dark shapes under the moonlight and that was all. It was obvious to me we were going to invade at night—I just didn't know when. Neither did Saddam.

Saddam was more concerned with security of his regime than he was concerned with an invasion, and he was more concerned with the American presence in Jordan and Syria than he was with the American presence in Kuwait. Incredibly, despite the loud noise we made in Kuwait feigning attacks across the border, he positioned the bulk of his troops around the capital, Baghdad. Maybe he realized that Iraq was indefensible at the borders, but it is also possible that since no-fly zones were in effect and the Air Force was bombing everything outside central Iraq, he decided his units would be safest in central Iraq. He also must have realized that as long as he and Baghdad stood, his regime had a future. Regime security trumped common sense. Saddam honestly thought that if the US invaded, they would encounter such a heroic defense that it would force the US to back down.

His logic was sound. America was used to limited warfare. He recalled the American experience in Vietnam, Bosnia, and Kosovo where public unrest convinced the American government to turn against war. He surmised that America would act the same if it invaded Iraq. With this logic, he also misunderstood the Iraqi people. He miscalculated that the Iraqi people would fight to the death for him and the regime.

Immediately before the invasion, Saddam's generals informed him about action at the Jordanian and Syrian border. He directed his generals to focus on a possible invasion from there. It totally distracted the regime from the real threat, which was US invasion from Kuwait. This worked to the advantage of Bravo Company and the rest of the tank crews from the Marines and the Army who were chomping at the bit to invade helpless Iraq. I was anxious, everyone was anxious. All our training led up to this moment.

A most unusual order was given to us before the invasion. *We were not to use Old Glory*. We were not to fly the American flag while in Iraq. To do so would make the Iraqis feel as if we were imperialists instead of liberators. To the Iraqis being fed by their propaganda machine, Americans and the coalition were a band of "outlaw imperialists." Marines were told that they were invading to liberate the Iraqi people, but there remained suspicion among the ranks that we were invading Iraq for some other less-than-honorable reason. No one knew what would become of Iraq after the invasion. It would certainly be an American asset in the Middle East, if not a territory by the war's end, a proposition not all Marines were on board with.

So, our flags were stowed ingloriously for the duration of the war. Sometimes we saw a tank or amtrack going full speed and the American flag flying in glory, but no matter who it was, a sergeant, lieutenant, or a colonel, they would eventually have to take it down and receive an ass-chewing for being so bold. I missed the flag. It motivated the hell out of us, and we barely saw it. It served a greater purpose with us fighting and dying under it than it did being hidden away as if it were contraband. It was our right as soldiers, and not the right of our leadership to deprive us of Old Glory.

Preparations were going smoothly as we waited at the dispersal area. As part of daily maintenance procedures on the M-88, I motioned the driver to move the M-88 forward as I pounded on the track links and tightened them with a ratchet. The low chugging of the twelve-cylinder, 1,500 horsepower engine overpowered the senses, but we were used to it.

The track was arguably the most important part of any tracked vehicle, and it needed daily attention. Also needing daily repetition was checking oil levels, banging sand out of air filters, and weapons maintenance. The M1 .50 caliber machine gun mounted at the top of the M-88 was constantly dirty, and no one bothered to clean it because we weren't supposed to be on the front lines. That oversight would come to haunt us later. We each maintained our M-16s, though, in reasonable order, as well as our M-9 pistols, probably because boot camp instilled in us a sense of pride in the condition of our personal weapons. Every tanker had duties like these, maintaining their respective M1-A1s; it's what made the tanker and Hercules crewman alike. Everyone at the dispersal area was maintaining their track and cleaning their weapons for what was to come.

Without warning, a voice echoed over the radio, "LIGHTNING!

LIGHTNING! LIGHTNING!" At the call, I hopped down into the M-88 and snatched up my gas mask. I knew what this meant. Saddam had launched a missile at us. I fumbled the mask more than I should have; the straps fought back in my struggle to ready them for my head. I cursed in all the commotion. Men quickly leapt in their respective vehicles, falling over their own feet, senses dulled by their masks. It was like being blindfolded. The Navy and the Air Force were in charge now, and we relied upon them to intercept the scud. Mask on, I slammed the hatch above me. The labored breathing slowly lulled me into a dead sleep. Hours passed. Waking to a general "unmask" call on the speaker, I peeled the rubber off the sweat on my face. The US Navy had begun launching Tomahawk cruise missiles at Baghdad. The scud missiles that Hussein had sent our way were rumored to be heading toward Kuwait City. *A strange move,* I thought. I assumed at the time that Saddam must have known where we were since we were making such a commotion at the border, but that was far from the truth. The missiles were intercepted nevertheless, turning out not to contain chemical agents—supposedly.

★ ★ ★ ★ ★

Sometime in the night, and before Operation Iraqi Freedom commenced on March 19, the Air Force launched a secret mission to discover the communications frequencies of the entire Iraqi military. The information about the flight was classified, but it most certainly happened judging by the full scope of US intelligence on the location of Saddam's units before and during the war. The reconnaissance aircraft used, a RC-135 V/W Rivet Joint, was an extensively modified C-135, according to information from the Air Force.[43] At an altitude of 50,000 feet, above the range of Saddam's weapons, it flew over Iraq and collected, in a matter of hours, all frequencies the Iraqi military

---

43 "RC-135V/W Rivet Joint," The United States Air Force, May 23, 2012, http://www.af.mil/AboutUs/FactSheets/Display/tabid/224/Article/104608/rc-135vw-rivet-joint.aspx

utilized. Simple decoding unlocked the frequencies. Iraqi radios were then turned against them. We knew exactly what the Iraqis were doing as they spoke unawares. Their locations were at our disposal by simple triangulation. It is uncertain whether Saddam Hussein knew, but it was soon clear that the Iraqis knew that we were listening.

The Al Nida Republican Guard Division, one of the best equipped units in the army, hid its artillery pieces in an orchard, the ammunition in another location, and the soldiers in a location they felt certain was safe from an air attack. The troops and division commander were completely stunned when a precision attack hit all three locations, annihilating the entire battalion.[44] Fear spread throughout the Iraqi military. The commander of a Republican Guard unit ordered his men to abandon their vehicles because the Americans seemed to know exactly where they were.[45] Precision bombing also demoralized soldiers, according to an Iraqi lieutenant general, who said, "The level of precision of attacks put real fear into the soldiers of the rest of the division. The Americans were able to induce fear throughout the army by using precision air power."[46]

Iraqi soldiers stopped sleeping near their vehicles and learned to construe any sign of a US air raid—the appearance overhead of a drone, the sound of a plane or the sudden explosion of a nearby tank—as a prompt to take cover.[47]

Communications throughout the army were restricted to landlines, and radio communications became limited. Entire divisions hid in fighting holes spread out in the desert or deserted in great numbers. To use the radio, to appear in the open, was suicide. The army therefore spread out and did not move, according to Lieutenant General Raad Hamdani. Staying concealed and maintaining radio

---

44 Woods, *Iraqi Perspectives Project*, 128.
45 Gordon, Michael R., and General Bernard E. Trainor, *Cobra II*, New York: Pantheon Books, 2006a. 412.
46 Lt. Gen. Majid Husayn Ali Ibrahim Al-Dulaymi in Woods, *Iraqi Perspectives Project*, 125.
47 McCarthy, Terry, "What Ever Happened to the Republican Guard?" *Time Magazine*, May 12, 2003. 39-40.

silence seemed the best strategy. Still there were successful precision attacks on the most concealed positions the moment a radio was used, causing mass carnage, and the attacks caused more movement, causing yet more carnage. The psychological effect was astounding. Soldiers from all branches deserted in droves as it became common knowledge that fighting the Americans was useless.

Helicopters outfitted with giant speakers whipped across the border not far from where I was, and I could almost hear the Metallica they were blasting in the darkness. Yes, Metallica. In order to frighten the Iraqis, the US military Psychological Operations Unit was relentless; the hammering guitar and growl of James Hetfield motivated the Marines. Since Vietnam, the US has deployed similar aircraft, or pole-mounted speakers pointing toward the enemy, to wear on their nerves—especially at night when a man's fears were at their greatest.

On the eve of battle, as the sun set on March 20, 2003, Major General James Mattis drafted a speech to all hands.

> For decades, Saddam Hussein has tortured, imprisoned, raped, and murdered the Iraqi people; invaded neighboring countries without provocation; and threatened the world with weapons of mass destruction. The time has come to end his reign of terror. On your young shoulders rest the hopes of mankind.
>
> When I give you the word, together we will cross the Line of Departure, close with those forces that choose to fight, and destroy them. Our fight is not with the Iraqi people, nor is it with members of the Iraqi army who choose to surrender. While we will move swiftly and aggressively against those who resist, we will treat all others with decency, demonstrating chivalry and soldierly compassion for people who have endured a lifetime under Saddam's

oppression.

Chemical attack, treachery, and use of the innocent as human shields can be expected, as can other unethical tactics. Take it all in stride. Be the hunter, not the hunted: never allow your unit to be caught with its guard down. Use good judgment and act in the best interests of our Nation.

You are part of the world's most feared and trusted force. Engage your brain before you engage your weapon. Share your courage with each other as we enter the uncertain terrain north of the Line of Departure. Keep faith in your comrades on your left and right and Marine Air overhead. Fight with a happy heart and strong spirit.

For the mission's sake, our country's sake, and the sake of the men who carried the Division's colors in past battles—who fought for life and never lost their nerve—carry out your mission and keep your honor clean. Demonstrate to the world there is "No Better Friend, No Worse Enemy" than a US Marine.

The order was given: move out at 2100.[48]

---

48   According to 2nd Tank Battalion's After Action Report, the Iron Horse crossed the border at 2110 (local time) on March 20. Some accounts vary from company to company because platoons of tanks crossed at different times, but for the purposes of history, the entire battalion which was leading RCT-5 was across by 2110. RCT-1 and RCT-7 led by 1st Tank Battalion crossed about a day later. RCT-5 was to remain one to two days in front of RCT-1, and RCT-7 throughout the invasion until it halted in northern Baghdad.

CHAPTER III

Invading Iraq

Laws are dumb in the midst of arms.

CICERO

OUT OF THE DARKNESS, 2nd Tank Battalion roared across the border, leading the charge for coalition forces.[49] An Iraqi minefield blocked one of the convoys but didn't slow Iron Horse for long. Tanks of Bravo Company leading RCT-5 (Regimental Combat Team 5) crawled through the breach-point. Bravo slowed to allow the other tank companies to catch up. Immediately, the night lit up in fire.

Hundreds of dismounted Iraqi soldiers aside eight scattered T-55s, two MT-LBs, and ten military vehicles attacked, and the Marines engaged them mercilessly. The giant 120 mm boomed from multiple American tanks, and within minutes all were smoking and the enemy killed or dying on the desert floor. They were no match for Alpha, Bravo, Charlie, and Delta Company's complement of fifty-eight M1-A1 Abrams tanks. The engaged fell quickly, and the tanks didn't bother to stop rolling right past them into the night.[50]

---

49 2nd Tank Battalion Command Chronology, 4.
50 Ibidem, 5.

A prayer was all that stood between myself and God. I shut my eyes and prayed that God would preserve me. It was a selfish pursuit. I should have flicked the switch on my helmet and asked everyone to join with me, but this prayer I said to myself. I could think of little else to do at the time, and I wish I could remember the words. I do recall, however, the emotions I felt and the echo of small arms and blast of tank fire just ahead. The track of Hells Wrecker moved up and down, slamming on the sand dune that separated Iraq from Kuwait. We lurched forward, my helmet knocking the front of my periscope, and I opened my eyes. *Fear.* I feared what was to come; we all did. In the midst of the chugging of the M-88, I focused on God while all around me Marines were saying "Here we go!" excited for the war ahead. We had waited in Kuwait for fifty-nine days, and we all were ready. We wanted to kill, flicking our communications switches in excitement at our crossing of the border.

RCT-5 with 2nd Tank Battalion in the lead were the first to cross the border to Iraq. RCT-1 led by Alpha Company, 1st Tank Battalion to the far left waited in silence at the border to move, and would not embark until the next day, and likewise for RCT-7 to the far-right flank led by the rest of 1st Tank Battalion. RCT-5 had a special mission. They raced through the desert, sometimes leaving their wagon trains lagging, and then slowed to allow them to catch up. We were in a race to capture the Rumaila oil fields located west of Basrah before Saddam could react. In the Gulf War he torched his oil fields, and there was no reason to think he would not do it again. The fields were the breadbasket of Iraq, producing millions of barrels of oil a day before the invasion, and Iraq would need them captured intact to recover afterward.

My job was to navigate the M-88 Hells Wrecker using my GPS device rigged directly from my seat in the M-88 to an external antenna on top of the hull. I was to inform the convoy officer of my coordinates every so often since the M-88 was in the rear of RCT-5, which would not last long. Maps lined the white walls inside of Hells Wrecker, directly in front of my seat. I followed with a pen our every move on the military maps under the green glow of the M-88's internal light. Our hatches were open, the desert breeze cooling the hot interior. I had a job to do that neither the driver nor the commander of the M-88 appreciated. Every hour, I transmitted our coordinates to the convoy officer of the day, who then relayed it to Colonel Dunford, commanding officer of RCT-5. Our M-88 was to be a tracked hospital in the event of mass casualties since we had ample room in the interior and exterior of the vehicle; hence, we carried a medic, a corpsman who popped his head out the rear-most hatch waiting for casualties. We all were armed and alert when crossing the border at 0300.

I poked my head out of the M-88 and felt a cool morning breeze. I gazed ahead and saw the dim outlines of the hummer directly in front of us, and the hummer in front of him. The tanks were not that far ahead. Suddenly, we received a call that we were needed on the front; a tank had gone down. We burst from our position in the convoy and raced toward the tank in distress at out maximum speed of 30 mph. In the moonless night, I saw the enormity of our convoy, of the 1st and 3rd Battalion, 5th Marines in amtracks and Humvees. As we passed through their lines, it struck me how much the invasion depended on order. If vehicles in the convoy deviated from course and began to cross one another, a royal mess of wheeled and tracked vehicles would slow our advance. Convoy commanders of RCT-5 synchronized their movements based upon the location of the tanks in front. I was glad not to be in their shoes.

Alone in the darkness, Hells Wrecker moved far from the convoy with expedience, led by the direction of my GPS. It wasn't long until the crew began to second-guess my interpretation of the GPS, and just as the commander ordered us back to the convoy, we saw a tank go muzzle-first into a ditch, helpless in the crossfire. Another Abrams came to the rescue, halting within a chain's length of the ditched monster. A Marine dismounted in the chaos, attempting to latch tow bars, and was forced back in the turret when a volley of rocket-propelled grenades (RPGs) sliced the air and ricocheted off the tank. Shadows in the moonlight was all that could be seen. The rest of the platoon moved to engage dismounted troops and left the stuck tank to fend for itself.

The tank's crew had plunged blindly at full speed into a ditch created by the Iraqi army to hide a tank up to the turret. Attempting to back up, the turbine engine whined, sand grinding along its frontmost tracks. The sand compacted, and the rear was the only section of the tank jutting out of the sand. After skillful maneuvering, the tank slammed level once again.

The Iraqi army had made dozens of tank ditches in the area to hide their ancient T-55's. The Iraqis knew that their armor could not stand up against the 120 mm main gun of an Abrams, so they made their tanks harder to see and harder to hit by hiding them in the dirt. Doing so made the tanks immobile, but it was the best chance they had. I saw the logic. The tankers punched the bore of the main gun, full of sand, and a mechanic within discovered no damage had been done. The fire had died down and I dismounted to help.

Eyes were wild at the news that the area north of the border was clear of enemy personnel. Cautious as always, our tanks proceeded far ahead of where Hells Wrecker waited. They moved steadily in columns through the border and encountered chaos only a few miles into Iraq. "Men fell like in a video game," one Marine told me. He was the gunner of his tank, and indeed, what he saw in his night-sights would have looked like a video game. Troops lay alongside camels and hot hulks of simmering iron. Death littered the field by the time I stepped foot upon it. Steaming bodies in the night. Most gaped at the moonlit carnage until the sergeants yelled to mount up.

The Russian-made T-55 tanks that had opened fire were surprisingly close. Of the thirty-five that sat in the southern desert, only about five had been occupied. The Iraqi tank crews had run away. The aged battalion didn't stand a chance against our modern destructive force. I imagined them fleeing into the desert night. They had waited to engage until they were close enough to see without night-sights under the grace of moonlight, and then they only got off a shot or so before they were destroyed by the Americans. Ancient Greek philosopher Hermocles said, "The true contempt of an invader is shown by deeds of valor in the field." There was fighting spirit in Iraq, as the few that remained were brave, I thought. Brave and dead.

Lance Corporal Bobby Hansford, a tank gunner from East Flat Rock, North Carolina, recounted the action of that moonless night:

> I remember that night well, I was 3rd platoon Bravo Company, I was on blue 2. It was so dark that night we could barely see with thermals, 3rd platoon was in the lead of Bravo Company, my tank was in front of third platoon, so my tank was in the lead of RCT-5 and Bravo as we went through the breach. We had a CD player hooked to the internal communications system playing the undertaker theme, we were all scared but didn't let it show. We all were taking caffeine pills like candy to stay alert. I remember when we got through the breach we went to staggered formation, that's when it happened, the first live incoming round. I remember my heart was about to beat out of my chest, this was it, no more shooting paper targets at sr10. This was the real deal, then the tank near us returned fire, I remember the muzzle flash through the thermals. As I said before it was so dark we could barely see, and we were all desperately trying to acquire targets as we were receiving fire. I caught a few faded heat signatures, too dark to tell what it was, first heat signature, target acquired! Fire! On the way! Boom. Still incoming, a herd of camels to the right of the first target, looked like troops running around them, sent bursts of coax through them. Still incoming, third heat signature, couldn't make it out,

fired on it, no more incoming. Never knew what it was, couldn't tell what it was, and we never actually knew who got the enemy until a couple of days later that last target I had was it.[51]

Battalion tanks ran low on fuel, and conveniently attached to our hulls were gigantic rubber fuel bladders. Holding hundreds of gallons of JP-8, each tank had a minimum of one apiece attached to the turret by cables. They weighed so much an entire crew couldn't lift them, and they were issued and filled before the invasion in anticipation of our initial sprint into Iraq. The rubber was extremely hard and could deflect most small arms, and it was pressurized, so filling the fuel tank was a simple matter of connecting a hose. Within forty-five minutes, and in the midst of sporadic enemy small arms fire, the Marines of 2nd Tank Battalion had successfully refueled, continuing the sprint to the Rumaila oil fields.

I looked out to the horizon and was awed by towers of flame in the distance. *The oil fields.* Some of them had been torched, sending flames hundreds of feet into the sky. I knew he would do it—Saddam wasn't above creating a cardiac arrest in his country. But how many had been torched? Were we too late? It was impossible to know, but at least six illuminated the sky. To the heavens, distant orbs of light followed south in perfect repetition, one after another. Flashes of red light intercepted the orbs, creating barely audible thumps. Scud missiles. Other Marines were also looking up.

"How did it come to this?" I whispered. So much had happened since 9/11, and here I was in southern Iraq under a symphony of chaos. The night, reflecting the red glow of fire, was full of destruction. Hells Wrecker returned to its place in the convoy, and the tankers, hopped up on caffeine pills, pressed ahead before more damage to the oil fields could be done.

---

51 Interview with Corporal Bobby Hansford, September 10, 2015, quoted from an email.

★ ★ ★ ★ ★

The next day came quickly. The lack of sleep bothered few of us; our adrenaline was through the roof from the night before. Behind the tanks, Hells Wrecker growled through the southern Iraqi countryside. Huge black tents accommodating large families dotted the desert. Goats grazed in weedy fields as their watchful shepherds remained close, the bland colors of fabric flapping in the breeze. Nomads. True Arabs living on forage in the desert gazed on the convoy; we gazed back.

As we rolled closer to our objective, enemy soldiers emerged from the dunes, surrendering in large numbers. The faces, the humbleness and the state of them I will never forget. Colonel Dunford, the commander of RCT-5, instructed us not to give the soldiers food or water. Supposedly, there were units in the Marine Corps dedicated to that specific task. Stored in the back of our M-88 were humanitarian rations meant to feed hungry Iraqis. I made out the faces of the surrendering soldiers with hands high in the air.

Hells Wrecker kicked up dust, sticking to my sweat. It settled on them, too, and their dark-green uniforms in the morning sun. Faces dark and thin, overworked and underfed, the Iraqi soldiers seemed to ignore the intimidating sight of the American convoy billowing dust alongside them. What struck me was how they carried themselves. As if unaware that they had uniforms on, they came close to our lines very innocently, like children, without fear in their eyes. They approached only with the desire to surrender peacefully. Getting closer now, I noticed that not a single element in our lines had tossed the soldiers anything. I deciphered their gestures, lifting hands to their mouths, tilting heads backward—they needed water. It was the only thing they absolutely needed, and I felt for them.

I looked to the commander of Hells Wrecker for a decision. I knew his thoughts were the same as mine. At his word, making sure nobody in our lines was watching, we pitched bottles upon bottles of water to the thirsty company. I was happy to see our water go to those who needed it more; the surprise and rejoicing in their faces will not soon leave my memory. The flat-green soldiers jumped and hooted. Some got down on their knees and praised God for such a gift. They chased the rolling bottles down and shouted, giving us thumbs-up and waving their hands frantically after us. To think that a person was to the point of giving praise for something so simple humbled me for some time—enemies showing each other respect. I waved back as our dust trail covered their faces, and the whole memory faded behind the billowing of our engine, satisfied we had done our part for humanity.

The M-88 made its way up to Highway 8, the first paved road we had seen since crossing the border. Slowly up the steep ramp we traced the exact trail of the tanks ahead. With a muffled thud, the Hercules track slapped against the sticky blacktop. As we accelerated to our top speed of thirty miles per hour, civilians appeared alongside the highway and at the rest stops. The convoy rudely decided to make its own path over the center lane, bending and flattening the center guards into the sand. We hooked up our CD player to the audio system and listened to Linkin Park as we destroyed the road. I was giddy the whole time. We had boldly made the decision to crush more of the center guides than was necessary when it came to be our turn to cross. There were no rules on these roads. Hell, it was the first time in our lives that we could do whatever we wanted on a major highway. The rage of the metal echoed in my soul.

The Rumaila oil fields crept into sight. Hells Wrecker rolled under flaming oil pipes whose smoke clouds touched the sky at a thousand feet. We passed dozens of massive, white gas-oil separators in the shape of farmers' silos. These were surrounded by large earthen mounds on all sides, most of them interconnected with small buildings and webs of tan pipes. Not a single civilian was in sight. Ceilings of charcoal-black smoke blocked the sun, choking us with stench. Word passed over the radio that the tanks ahead of us had come in contact with enemy tanks and scattered troops. They had made it to the bridge. Were we too late? The radio hummed and barked messages that the Iraqi tanks were staged on the other side, waiting. The bridge was still intact. This had become a race. The ball had been dropped in the center of the theater, and a race to the middle ensued for the precious chance at the upper hand.

Over the radio I heard something extraordinary. It was the first order I know of for "recon by fire."[52] This meant *any* suspicious targets were first engaged with a weapon of choice *before* they could be positively identified. It went directly against the military's rules of engagement requiring that a soldier *must* identify his target *before* he attacks it. It is an affront to the limited warfare that the United States has been fighting since Vietnam, and arguably since the Korean War, where we commonly let the enemy "get the drop on us," giving him just a few extra seconds while we digested his intentions. To the Marines, "recon by fire" meant a field day, a free-for-all. It meant total-war. It motivated the crap out of us as we searched out the enemy without regard to consequence. We were not complicit; the order came from the top. The result, in Bravo Company alone, was six D-30 artillery pieces destroyed, two bunkers, three T-55s destroyed, two ZSU 23-4s destroyed, one destroyed technical vehicle, one Iraqi patrol boat, and a sniper while taking Rumaila.[53] Other companies were successful, but it is not known if they utilized "recon by fire." The death order was to be used sporadically, and effectively, throughout the rest of the campaign with awesome results.[54]

The infantry unloaded from the AAVs into an intense firefight at Pumping Station Two just south of us, incurring casualties, the first

---

52 Company B After Action Report, 2.
53 Ibidem. Though it is not in the records, a certain Lance Corporal Stinson fired at a silhouette on the top of a gas-oil separator and killed him; he retrieved the weapon afterwards to show us that he killed a sniper.
54 It was used with awesome results both good and bad. Bad namely because often civilians would be harmed in the action; my experience with Bravo on March 27 is just one small example where Marines and soldiers used "recon by fire" to ill effect. More examples exist, though it has been my experience that few Marines and soldiers talk openly about them.

RCT-5 saw in the war.[55] AAVs that followed immediately behind the Abrams opened their hatches, spilling Marines onto the battlefield in greater numbers than any other American force. What made the Marines different was their classification as an invasion force—not an occupying one. Invasion was what Marines were trained to do, and they proved extremely effective. When a tank in front became engaged, the entire column staggered left or right depending on the direction of the threat, AAVs unloading Marines onto the field in line with the heavy cavalry. This unsafe and aggressive gesture of force is precisely what caught the lesser-trained Iraqi regular or militiaman off guard. And perhaps the weak armor of the AAV also got the Marines on the field. Better to die on one's well-trained feet than roast in a twenty-nine-ton hulk.

As the tanks and amtracks full of infantry made their way up to the cream-colored silos, fire spilled from warped openings. Oily flames covered the access road, which ran directly through the facility, with smoke so black it canceled out the sun. The roads were also covered in mines, in potholes cut in the asphalt. We ran directly over them, and by the grace of God they did not explode. The Iraqi forces loved explosives and used them to partially destroy the facility that produced approximately 1.3 million barrels of oil a day before the war.[56] We were directed to preserve the silos and prevent, if possible, their destruction by the enemy. In that most crucial objective to our mission, we failed.

The far-reaching importance of the seizure of the southern and northern Rumaila gas-oil separators and oil storage complex knew no bounds. It was second to none in the entire country; the Kirkuk facility in northern Iraq producing 700,000 barrels a day was the only one that came close.[57] According to the *Oil and Gas Journal Study on*

---

55 Regimental Combat Team 5 Narrative Summary, United States Marine Corps, actions of March 20-21.
56 Erik Kriel, *Energy Information Administration Country Analysis Briefs: Iraq*, June 2006, http://lugar.senate.gov/issues/foreign/iraq/pdf/13_EIA_Iraq_CAB.pdf
57 Ibidem.

International Petroleum, beneath Iraq's sand and the famous Tigris and Euphrates, which snake the country, lie 115 billion barrels of proven oil reserves, sixty-five percent of which are in southern Iraq alone—the land the Marines just conquered.[58] The hard power we issued to the Iraqi Army was dwarfed by the benefits corporations would reap and had already reaped in business deals leading up to—and after— the war. The US government contracted to Kellogg Brown & Root, a subsidiary of Halliburton, to deal with the blazing gas-oil separators and oil fields the Marines so proudly secured. The contract was worth approximately seven billion dollars to the Texas-based company, which was about to have a hell of a time.[59] From April 2003 to 2006, there were a recorded 315 militant attacks upon Iraq's oil pipeline system and power grid, causing a substantial loss in oil production.[60] The power vacuum also generated business for a South African security company, Erinys International, which was part of a $100 million contract to train and arm 14,000 security guards to combat a growing insurgency. OPEC was another source of anxiety in the global arena. Besides Saudi Arabia and Canada, Iraq has the third largest proven oil reserve in the world, and if OPEC desired to retaliate against the war by replacing the American dollar with the euro, which had been established January 1, 2002, there could be other hostilities.[61] But these were worries for a different time; for now the liberating Marines peppered the silos, hunting for the enemy.

Some distance on the other side of the precious bridge, two enemy tanks lay smoldering from the surprisingly quick attack from US Apache helicopters. The choppers swooped overhead, governing the skies like a mob of angry wasps. Nine M1-A1 tanks spread on the left and right of the US-controlled side provided fire to secure the bridge from Iraqi harassment. A ZSU-23-4 was spotted across the Saddam Canal. Its large anti-aircraft turret poking through the brush was easily

---

58   Kriel, *Energy Information*.
59   Kellogg Brown & Root, http://www.kbr.com
60   Kriel, *Energy Information*.
61   Perkins, *Confessions*, 251.

recognizable by its four .23 caliber barrels pointed toward the sky. One of our tanks slammed it with a main gun round. Its metal hull exploded in a blast of fire; smoke steamed over the miserable pieces. To my surprise, word sounded over the radio that Hells Wrecker was needed up at the bridge. Was a tank hit? We were never sure until boots hit the ground, and we had no idea as we maneuvered past the convoy up to the bridge that we were to remain on the front line from that point on with Captain Gunn as he pushed ahead.

I remained excited as the bridge came into view. I watched as the Apaches unleashed hell on enemy forces that unwisely left the safety of foxholes. Some fled in panic from smoking tanks that had been hit. In their search for ground units, the dozen or so Apache helicopters displayed incredible strategy, perfectly passing one another in a weaving pattern which quickly brought them past the bridge to the other side. I found amazing the speed at which they were able to move in constant alignment.

Bombers made their distinct howl above the clouds as Hells Wrecker moved into position far on the left flank. Smoke rose in the north, and by the muffled pings I knew the smoke came from the payload issued from aircraft above. Saddam had not destroyed the bridge, but he could not have been stupid enough to leave it at our disposal. I remained cautious. The thuds in the distance ceased. The helicopters seemed to have eliminated the threat, circling back behind our lines. I glanced around and rose out of my hatch to get a better look at what we had accomplished.

The land was a mottled trash heap. Jutting out of the soft, loose earth were rusted trucks and other various military equipment destroyed ten years earlier in the first Gulf War. The Saddam Canal was filled with this same trash. Cattails overwhelmed the ugliness of them for the moment, but their presence loomed. Stagnant ponds lay about, brimming with mosquitoes, and the stench of pollution stretched the nostril like a disease. This was an overflow area. An earthen rise in front of the tanks made to hold the canal in place made a perfect protective barrier; turrets poked just above the threshold, providing protection and maximum view. The Rumaila Bridge was perhaps fifty yards across and built with huge concrete supports that could easily hold a seventy-ton tank. Our tanks had been firing at suspicious targets on the east side of the bridge, out of sight of Hells Wrecker, using small caliber weapons, so I eased up a little and took off my helmet. The afternoon wind felt cool against my sweaty forehead. I closed my eyes and tried to relax under the midday sun.

Without warning, a deafening blast shook the Hercules on the stable ground, and the crew, who had been relaxing with hatches open, dove inside. Whipping around, I was amazed to see two billowing clouds of smoke descending from the opposite side of the bridge. A section of it split, muffled by the blast, sending it plummeting into the shallow water below. I sat dumbfounded, staring at the section of the bridge in the water leaning against its other half in a giant V. The Rumaila Bridge had been detonated. I hastily strapped on my helmet, readying myself for another blast. I felt helpless like the poor Iraqi units in Baghdad who had been mercilessly bombed nights before—like a target. The inch-thick walls about me could never counter a blast like that. Everyone in the surrounding tanks was just as stunned as I.

The remaining forces on the other side had completed their ultimate mission. American troops could still easily cross, but no longer the tanks. It is what they wanted—to keep the American armor out. The utter importance of the bridge struck me. Now we would need to head west and attempt to cross the Euphrates River. To my knowledge the stability of the other crossings was questionable. The dust settled on the still water below the wreck, and Marines slowly relaxed. Mr. Hussein had won this race.

★ ★ ★ ★ ★

It was noon on March 21, and RCT-1 and RCT-7 had begun their march up from Kuwait. RCT-7 was sprinting to secure the multibillion-dollar Az Zubayr oil pumping station. Oil from 300 of 454 active wells at Rumaila flowed through it, generating $40 million a day for the Iraqi people. The pumping station was as important as the oil fields themselves.[62] British and American Marines had already seized the Al Faw oil manifolds at the port Umm Qasr, also vital to Iraq's oil infrastructure.

Task Force Tarawa, led by a platoon of tanks from Alpha Company, 8th Tank Battalion, began its run to secure the Jalibah Airfield west of Rumaila. We were a half day north of them. Delta tanks in front of 3rd Battalion, 5th Marines had secured three gas-oil separation plants (GOSP) with just a few casualties. Bravo, leading 2nd Battalion, 5th Marines, secured a fourth. RCT-5 claimed Rumaila with little resistance, "covering 70 kilometers of territory mostly under the cover of darkness, in ten hours."[63] The Army 3rd Infantry Division, with its complement of 200 M1-A1 tanks, began its long run through the desert to An Nasiriyah to seize the Tallil Air Base and As Samwah to isolate the Fedayeen and Ba'ath militia there.[64] With their 120 Challenger 2 main battle tanks and 150 Warrior infantry fighting vehicles, the British started their run to seize the Iraqi main port of Basra. They were closing in on the outskirts, allowing civilians to escape town. The grand movements of the coalition were but markings on a map; Iron Horse focused on what we immediately controlled—the ground we sat on, and the maximum range of our main guns.

Muffled blasts beyond the bridge had long since died. The aura of anxiety subsided to a comfortable level. Mosquitoes began the morbid task of eating us to the point of near insanity. I stepped off Hells Wrecker, finding ease in walking up the embankment on which

---

62 West, Bing, and Major General Ray L. Smith, *The March Up: Taking Baghdad with the United States Marines*, Bantam: 2004, 15.
63 2nd Tank Battalion Command Chronology, 5.
64 Colonel Fontenot, Gregory, Lt. Col. E.J. Degen, and Lt. Col. David Tohn, *On Point: The United States Army in Operation Iraqi Freedom*, Combat Studies Institute Press, 2004: Fort Leavenworth, KS, 88.

the M-88 and other tanks had been perched. Ignoring the danger that an enemy could easily see my silhouette, I passed large hulks of rusty Jeep and truck metal.

The stagnant Saddam River stunk amid clusters of tall grass and oily yellow surface slime. There was a commotion ahead toward the bridge. I sped my pace, catching sight of Captain Gunn giving orders to troops. Coming into view next to his tank were two men. My foot struck a pile of AK-47s, gas masks and ammunition taken from the enemy. I looked to them, then to the pile. Was this all they had carried with them? No food, no extra clothes, no hygiene equipment, no money? I stepped over the small heap to a few Marines who gathered to gawk at the catch of the day.

I saw the prisoner attempting to communicate. Comprehending nothing of the Arabic words intermixed with his body language, I studied his actions. Placing both hands on his chest, an officer patted himself as if to say, "I" or "Me." Then he brought both skinny hands to his chin, made an *L* with both his thumb and index finger on either hand. He then commenced to point left, with his thumbs sticking straight up, and jerked his arms back vigorously as if shooting a rifle. Then, dropping one arm to his side, he pointed the other high to the clear blue sky and uttered one word, "Allah."

The Marines looked at each other in complete understanding. He fought for Allah. Some, in disbelief, scoffed at the realization of his intentions; the man's companion, huddling close to him, stared nervously at the Americans. To the Marines, a gun was a gun; whether the cause was honorable in the eyes of the combatant had no significance. He and his companion were the enemy, and in the belief of our enemy, *the Americans* were Allah's enemy.

The Marines chuckled and joked at the newfound piety of the prisoner, failing to realize the deep meaning in the message. I studied the man who had just communicated with us. Around six feet tall, the Iraqi major was balding, possibly in his mid-thirties, wearing tattered clothes that hid his lanky form like a curtain. Shoes falling apart due to wear, hands bone-bare, tan, weathered skin wrapping them as tight as leather hide, a white-and-grey, unshaven face under clearly tired, bagged eyes, he brought his forearms to the middle of his body and crossed them repeatedly, shaking his head side to side. Finally, pointing north across the river he spoke. "Saddam." *Not Saddam*, he gestured.

"So, that makes him innocent," the Marine next to me blurted. One of the guards motioned to the Iraqis to sit. From one of the tanks, two humanitarian ration meals were handed to a corporal, who took the two meals to the men. He held them out, one in each hand; the prisoners accepted them slowly. The corporal brought his fingers to chin and waved his hand to his mouth, saying, "Eat."

The men looked down to the large, bright packages in their hands and then back to the corporal. The Iraqi major touched his meal and his eyes grew wet, tears running down his cheeks. His face cupped in his weary hands, he spoke in low tones, sobbing in happiness for the gift of sustenance. Lifting his hands toward heaven and muttering words to Allah, he choked and praised; the quiet one sat dumbfounded at his gift.

After some time, my gaze met the major's piercing blue eyes, uncommon to the peoples here. His gaze was pure, unafraid. His gesture echoed in my thoughts thereafter: "I fight for Allah." I wondered if his God saw us as his enemy. Certainly every one of the Marines looked upon the two Iraqis as such. "Soldiers of Allah," I whispered; we were infidels, after all.

RCT-5 processed hundreds of prisoners of war over the next twelve hours; a brigade-sized enemy force was all that protected Rumaila from the invaders.[65]

That night, the stars were brilliant. The Milky Way shone clearer than I had ever seen before with my naked eye. This was a precious time. I was tired. No sleep from the night before had drained me

---

[65] Regimental Combat Team 5 Narrative Summary, United States Marine Corps, actions of March 20-21.

and the rest of the crew, who were passed out. We enjoyed the safety of the tanks keeping watch all night, so we did not have to worry. I eventually fell into a deep sleep on the spade of the M-88, looking up at the heavens.

I jumped a foot in my sleeping bag, awakened by a deafening burst of .50 caliber fire. I tore the bag off my face and gaped toward the sound. The tank directly in front of us must have spotted something on the other side of the canal; more "recon by fire." I laid my head back down in relief that the racket hadn't come from the enemy. They engaged until morning, pissing me off every time. Like an idiot, I insisted on sleeping outside in spite of all that occurred. The others rested in the M-88; I doubt the noise woke them. The mosquitoes relished this place as well. I heard the swarms hum between live fire. Swatting them from my sleeping bag, I erected a shelter to save myself a swollen face in the morning.

The next day, we left the ugly maze of pipes and silos to the protection of the 3rd Parachute Battalion and the 16th Air Assault Brigade of the 1st United Kingdom Army Division. We scarcely got a chance to associate with our allies and never saw the blazing complex again.[66] To the Marines, it was an objective accomplished; to the world it was oil saved. *Oil*. Was it for Iraq or for us? I didn't know at the time. But the Marines spoke of oil, as did the rest of America, as if it were our goal. The grand movements of the coalition suggested that, for the time being, our priority was oil. At the time I had my suspicions, but I was also a capitalist. If we did want the oil for ourselves and the world, we had done a marvelous job in securing it.

We left the destroyed bridge, rolling west on Highway 8 to cross the Euphrates at Highway 1 to the north, a journey of approximately 100 kilometers. It was unclear to me how we would guarantee the bridge remained intact for our crossing. There was no reason to believe that Saddam would not destroy that bridge as well.

We endured a tactical road march the next day. No one knew

---

66 Company B.

what to expect of the Iraqi forces. They should have defended Rumaila better for the good of their country if nothing else. The lack of enemy forces in the south indicated that they were concentrated in the north; that was what we were all thinking, even if nobody was saying it. They were in fact concentrated in and around Baghdad, primarily along the Iranian border in the event their neighbors decided to take advantage of the situation. We wisely avoided the border, cutting up the middle along Highway 1—the fastest route to Baghdad. It was hard to know what to expect.

The movements of the Iraqi Army were clandestine to most Marines of low rank. Many were without communications, without maps, without knowledge of the country we were invading. They rolled through the war, awakened by the occasional pop of Iraqi fire or spilling out when ordered to a tactical situation that demanded the Marines to kill. I was unlike these men.

Sitting in Hells Wrecker, I enjoyed a periscopic view of the war, lifting my chair to breathe the thin Iraqi air whenever I pleased and tracking RCT-5 as it made its way north slowly, thirty miles per hour at best. The green interior lights of the M-88 comforted me, as did the rifle at my side, as did the chugging of the engine. I switched driving from time to time to allow the crew to sleep, taking in the mundane movement of the M-88 to relax my mind. Rest the night before at Rumaila did little for me, wishing I had the caffeine pills my tanker counterparts did as I drove north.

★ ★ ★ ★ ★

Toward the evening on the twenty-third, we entered the city of An Nasiriyah with no intelligence whatsoever. Our route took us slowly through dirt streets lined with small mud-brick and concrete buildings with canvas flaps for doors. I peered out my hatch and noticed that there were no civilians walking about. It was eerie when combined with the orange light coming from the west, and we had almost made it through when we heard gunfire ahead. Over the radio a voice ordered us to "button up," and we quickly closed our hatches, looking through our periscopic windows to the dead city. It was hard to know what to do in the Hercules as we could not engage the enemy from inside. So, we sat nervously listening to the firefight. A few minutes later we were pelted with enemy bullets rattling on the hull. It sounded like rain on a tin roof. Our backs stiffened and we looked at each other in surprise, not knowing what to do as the tankers ahead engaged their targets. It was the first time we had been directly shot at. We crawled at ten miles per hour through the hot zone until it stopped. We were not to become entangled in Nasiriyah—that was obvious. We left it behind for someone else to deal with. I appreciated the Hercules. I felt relatively safe, forgetful that the enemy could have RPGs, which would easily penetrate our inch-thick hull.

We averaged 100 km a day on the front. As the sun set on the twenty-third, I was ready for a change. We survived by rotating drivers the whole while and were generally tired and bored from inactivity and the slow march. I was surprised as the bridge east of An Nasiriyah came into view.

It had been a mystery to me how we would take the bridge intact as the Iraqi Army must have known our intentions. Securing the bridge before we arrived was no less than 3rd LAR (light armored reconnaissance), commanded by Lt. Col. Stacy Clardy from RCT-7. They had endured an exhausting high-speed tactical march from As Zubayr, skirting Highway 8 to the juncture of Highway 1, passing everybody on the road to make a lightning attack on the bridge to secure it for the slower-moving RCT-5. Known as the "Wolfpack," 3rd LAR consisted of approximately sixty LAV-25s (light armored vehicles) with 25 mm chain guns on the turrets and two M240 7.62 mm machine guns in support. They were light tanks made extremely useful by their operational range of 600 km and their top speed of approximately 100 kmh. They came in no less than eight variants, such as the LAV-AT anti-tank version, the LAV-M mortar version, and the LAV-R recovery version, which made LAR adaptable to almost any combat situation. They had engaged and destroyed a battalion-sized force before we arrived and secured the bridge without losing a man. After crossing, we attached them to RCT-5 and pressed forward through the night.

Hundreds of flickering infrared bulbs passed through my night vision goggles. Ghostly lines of stopped tanks huddled close in the darkness. Taking the goggles slowly from my eyes, I admired the silence. Nothing was discernable without the use of night vision technology. I stood erect out of my hatch, taking advantage of the moment. In the utter blackness we waited for the command to start our engines and keep moving. It was out there—a ruin that I knew well from history books, something I could only wish to see in daylight, trying to picture its subtle outlines in the impossible darkness. Ur, the oldest city of the ancient Sumerian civilization, home of Abraham. Only glimpsing it in books, my curiosity had to stop there as I was confined to the security of Hells Wrecker. My imagination placed our elusive enemy there. Pitted eyes hidden under dirty helmets, dug in with ancient bricks—better to gaze upon it from the mind's eye than travel afoot to it, to my death. A cold chill swept across me, creeping up my spine.

News had been circulating based on reliable sources. Earlier in the morning on March 23, soldiers from 507th Maintenance Company of the 5th Battalion, 52nd Air Defense Artillery took a wrong turn into An Nasiriyah, which was still occupied by the enemy. They were ambushed in a hail of fire, dragged from their vehicles, bound and gagged. Many were shot execution style. Shot like animals. A woman, PFC Jessica Lynch, was taken prisoner with many others.[67] I felt anger boil and a terrible sense of awareness as all this was happening just east of us. We had bypassed An Nasiriyah in the night, and the more vulnerable units behind the tanks were left for the picking. In a flash, I saw myself bound like my compatriots, felt the helplessness as they fell, saw the darkness behind a blindfold.

---

67   Fontenot, *On Point*, 89.

Task Force Tarawa was held up in An Nasiriyah as well. They saw a bloody day, losing eighteen Marines in bitter street fighting with many more injured trying to secure two key bridges there. The cost of our easy passage through town struck me as the flaw of our invasion doctrine. Speeding to Baghdad was manifesting collateral damage. It was a dark day for the coalition, and although Tarawa was supported by Alpha Company, 8th Tank Battalion, they were bogged down trying to secure the town, making the ultimate sacrifice. Morale of every unit that had knowledge of An Nasiriyah was shaken, even to the highest echelons at CFLCC (the coalition forces land component command). If it was this difficult to secure a town in the south, how much harder would it be to take Baghdad?[68]

The coalition made its first strike at the Karbala Gap on the twenty-third, and it too was a dismal failure. The 11th Attack Helicopter Regiment sent a wave of Apache AH-64 helicopters to Karbala; thirty returned riddled with bullet holes. The Iraqi Medina and Nebuchadnezzar Division were no doubt caught off guard, but they quickly recovered, shooting one Apache down and taking two warrant officers prisoner. The attack did little damage to the defenders and did much to the psyche of the coalition. It was an Iraqi victory. News reached my ears sporadically; I did not grasp at the time how dark a day it was for the coalition. RCT-5, however, squeezed through while most others were held up in and around An Nasiriyah, including RCT-1, who was trying to head up Highway 7 to form the right flank of the giant pincer that was part of our strategy.[69]

The air died down, reduced its bite to an uneasy stillness. What would this night bring for us? Our giant columns of vehicles were

---

68 An entire book has been written about the Marines and the battle for An Nasiriyah on the twenty-third of March. It is in-depth and riveting. Prichard, Tim, *Ambush Alley: The Most Extraordinary Battle of the Iraq War*, Presidio Press: 2007.
69 Putting together the pieces of information about troop movements on the twenty-third is extremely difficult. The roads were clogged, the Army and Marines were crossing lines, and various bridges in An Nasiriyah were contested. I have deliberately left out some movements so as to lessen the confusion. That day was a quagmire in the initial sprint into Iraq. God knows how CFLCC dealt with it.

impossible to see unless one marched headlong into them. I forcefully shook my head. My mind was drifting; I was tired. It did strike me that there yet remained a sizeable military force in Iraq, with the latest estimate around 200,000. As for our military in general—we didn't know the true ability of our enemy, how many remained loyal to their cause. This startled me. We were walking into something blindly, expecting ease of passage all the way to Baghdad, the truth in numbers as bleak as the moonless night above me.

★ ★ ★ ★ ★

Close to Ad Diwaniyah on Highway 1 on March 25, 3rd Battalion, 5th Marines ran into trouble, pinned down by a surprisingly coordinated ambush. In a hail of automatic machine gun fire, First Lieutenant Brian R. Chontosh commanded his vehicle to drive off the road, straight toward Iraqi trenches. RPGs and mortars sliced the air as he rolled up to the enemy, where he dismounted and emptied his ammunition, killing, with the help of a single other Marine, over twenty Iraqi fighters. "It's nothing like TV," Chontosh told a reporter at *Newsweek*. "It's ugly. It's contorted. People fall how they fall. It's not like the bullet hits and they're blown back or anything like that."[70] The fight was so intense they were obliged to pick up Iraqi weapons, silencing a greater part of the battlefield and making safe the rest of the convoy. The stiff firefight was within earshot as the convoy moved slowly north, and the lieutenant later received the Navy Cross and two Bronze Stars for his heroism in the face of heavy fire that day.[71]

Back at my position, the sky changed from bright blue to a dusty, thick orange. Standing outside the M-88, sand brushed gently against my face. Since making our way west from Rumaila and north past An Nasiriyah and Ur to our current position east of Ad Diwaniyah,

---
70 http://www.wearethemighty.com/military-stories-movies-2015-...
71 Full Text Navy Cross Citation of 1st Lieutenant Brian R. Chontosh, Home of Heroes, Newsweek interview of Brian Chontosh. http://homeofheroes.com/members/02_NX/citations/09_GWOT/nc_21wot_USMC.html, accessed March 10, 2017.

we had traveled primarily under the cover of darkness. Conserving energy during the day, running the columns ever northward at night had taken its toll. Days and nights blended together as one memory, one giant day full of events that one could scarcely track. The heat of day did not lend itself to sleep, nor did the Marines favor living in a nocturnal state. The orange sky signaled the precursor to a sandstorm. In the lull between movement, I took time to pen a thought in my journal:

> It seemed like a dream; one of those that you could not discern from fantasy or reality. Like a fairy tale, how they depict the surroundings totally foreign and unique from ours. I have never before seen skies like this.[72]

Hopping up on Hells Wrecker, I assumed the machine gun position on the sweltering commander's hatch. The storm came slowly, the M-88 sealed to prevent the dust from raiding the inside. I sat on top alone, standing watch behind my .50 caliber. Fastening helmet and fixing my goggles for the onslaught, I waited. "This damn M2!" I swore aloud. "If they only could fire from the inside!" These thoughts did not save me. A tidal wave of sand clawed its way toward me, engulfing all in its path, so fierce it appeared to have purpose. Papers and light pieces of garbage accompanying the storm could well have traveled hundreds of miles to where I sat now. It surrounded me.

I pursed my lips and suddenly realized it would be impossible to make a shot in any direction to defend myself. I had underestimated this storm; I attempted to see the hand in front of my face. Quickly tying a bandanna around my sand-salted mouth, I realized that every crevice of my person would be invaded with sand. I accepted my fate, sitting like I had not a moveable joint in my body, like a worthless lump on a gigantic log. My mind wandered, peaceful with the lack of

---

72   Corporal Grant, Aaron, *Journal from March 2,3 2003-December 21, 2005*, 16.

sight. In the rush of wind and orange earth, I pictured—though I don't understand why—being in a different place at another time. Images of the ancient armies of Sargon the Great and the mighty Hammurabi came to me, marching in this same parched land. Their faces blasted like my own, salty rings around thousands of dry mouths. This sand carried their story. I envisioned history in the grit between my teeth. A powerful wind slammed my body; I looked down through my green-tinted goggles to my person. No difference in fabric, only a flat shelf of orange. I had become a dune. Though the sand encroached into my uniform at an incredible rate, I sat still.

The storm was almost over. I could see again, forcing imagination back down to earth. I stood, the sand rolling off my hands as fast as it came. The scattered trash that the convoy produced had been carried along with the storm, its sole companion for another hundred miles. The storm encompassed the entire theater of operations for about an hour.

God has always used the weather to intervene in human events. I later discovered that satellite images from that exact time picked up extensive enemy movement while the entire coalition remained still. It was no simple act of nature. What was foiled because of the sandstorm, or what was done because of it, had infinite possibilities. Recalling a story from the Revolutionary War, I remembered how George Washington and his retreating army crossed the East River in the Battle of Brooklyn Heights in 1776. He took advantage of the night to move his army in boats across the river to Manhattan but didn't have nearly enough time to complete the task. At dawn, a deep fog suddenly settled, so thick one could barely see a foot in any direction. The British, hot on his heels, could do nothing but wait it out. By the time it lifted, the Americans had long crossed the river in one of the greatest, most organized military retreats in history, saving nearly 10,000 Americans and the revolution itself. Thanks to God, and God only. It was apparent God was doing the same in this war, lifting the enemy from bunkers and foxholes so we could engage after the weather cleared. It also allowed the Iraqis to adapt to their perilous situation without harassment from us. God designs the outcome of battles.

Around this time, a blessing landed on Hells Wrecker. Hearing a commotion on back of the M-88, I looked back and met the gaze of a pigeon under the orange sky. I wasn't surprised until he hopped down into the commander's hatch. The shining purple-and-pale-grey creature searched, oblivious to all of us inside staring at it. Up until that point, I had not seen a single bird in Iraq, and here one was acting like it had brain damage, nestling into a cap hanging on the bulkhead. He fluffed himself up, circled a few times, and fell asleep. And there he stayed for three days. He became "Willie," and he let us pet him, feed him, put him on our shoulders, and every evening he would return to his cap and fall asleep when we did. Writing in my journal about him, I knew he was more than he seemed:

> In the direction I was looking, a pigeon landed on the tank. Some people see things as a simple coincidence, an act of chance. Others see it as more of a chance; they see a sign. I am the latter, and this fearless creature is a sign. My spirit, as of late, has run too fast. Too little time to focus and see like I normally do. "He's probably someone's pet" I tell myself. He reminds me of how simple life can be, and how content you can be if you let yourself. Who knows when he'll leave; for the time being I will enjoy his company as he does mine.[73]

For the days we had him, Willie reminded me to be content. Looking at him sleeping in the smelly Hercules, regardless of the firefights, he made me think of faith. *Have faith.* God would teach me later in life to be content, and I see now he sent this messenger to

---

73 Grant, Journal, March 23, 2003-December 21, 2005, 18.

show us all that if a bird, who we could squash at any time, could be content with us, then we should be content and have faith we could deal with a few Iraqis.

> *Faith is to believe what you do not see; the reward of this faith is to see what you believe.*
> **SAINT AUGUSTINE**

The sandstorm cleared, and Bravo Company spotted a civilian vehicle coming directly at them on the highway, traveling at a high rate of speed. The tanks fired a warning shot with small arms. No reaction. The vehicle sped directly for us. We tensed as we surmised the car could be packed with explosives. Another shot was fired. This time it ricocheted off the pavement directly in front of the car and buried itself in the chest of the passenger. The car wheeled and arced to a complete stop directly in front of the tanks. Tankers dismounted and pulled the wounded driver from the car. He was a deserter, and the man with a gaping hole in his chest was his uncle. "Why didn't you stop!?" screamed the Marines.

No one could understand what he was blubbering. The man sitting dead in the seat caused the Marines to shout obscenities. He wasn't a combatant, and there he was dead, and the deserter crying. No one could figure out why they were moving so fast directly for the tanks. They had no explosives or firearms. They were afraid of something ahead. Pulling the dead man from the car, someone produced a tarp to drape over him, and there he lay for days. I looked at his lifeless arm dangling with a wedding ring on it. *What an idiot,* I thought. *What were you running from?*

I had a good idea why they were running. There was not a single friendly unit ahead of us. There were artillery strikes, 2,000 sorties by Apache helicopters, jets, and bombers, and Baghdad had been hit by cruise missiles. The Army was currently fighting in As Samwah, west of An Nasiriyah, and Najaf to the west of Ad Diwaniyah, and securing local airfields. If that didn't make the deserter flee, it was the Ba'ath militia or Fedayeen, who forced Iraqi troops to fight, that scared the hell out of them. In either case, the deserter and his uncle found making a suicidal run toward the American tanks preferable to what lay ahead.

And there was *something* ahead.

CHAPTER IV

Everything Changes

If his cause be wrong, Our obedience to the King wipes the crime of it out of us.
WILLIAM SHAKESPEARE, HENRY V

ON THE CRISP MORNING of March 27, we passed countless homes made of mud brick, their occupants gazing from within with innocent eyes. Occasionally, following in slow pace with the tanks, we were entertained by crowds of civilians gathered to watch the fabled US Marines. They were as unknown to us as any outsider in the context of war. I had been told that the Iraqis believed that killing someone was part of Marine Corps recruit training. They thought we were bloodthirsty, though most had never killed anyone. Arab faces thrust from every corner. I was amazed at their quietness, the colors, their mystery. I cursed myself for not learning Arabic in Kuwait where I had plenty of time to do so. It was not only the culture that was shocking but also not knowing what information they had of the enemy's movements around us. If we just could communicate with the civilians, the invasion would have been easier. Light eyes hidden under a purple veil here, small children whispering to one another there. I sensed questioning hearts.

The Marines in Iraq were like a closed society—a counterculture even—with its own values and language floating about the desert. It was impossible to know the Iraqi through the lens of Americanism, which clashed directly with Iraqi nationalism. Truly, if not for the ever-present language barrier, we could get over the rest.

The language killed us and the culture shocked us. We did not know that the Iraqi was fiercely tribal, that his loyalty was to his neighbor, not Saddam, though he wouldn't speak of it to avoid the secret police. Could the Marines—the wolfpack, the counterculture— truly understand the Iraqi? We understood tactics, the bullets flying, and the bombs. From that alone we understood the motivation—and ineptitude—of the Iraqi military. But outside of that, the civilians hiding in the shadows or squatting beneath trees were an enigma. An us-and-them complex developed very quickly, as if the people were beyond understanding. It was convenient. When we looked at *them* it was easier to see something less than a human being, an enemy who was simply waiting for the opportunity to strike, informing his friends on our movements, taking advantage of the language barrier to hide his true intentions. Yes, the Iraqis were a finger's touch away from us and couldn't be farther at the same time. They became objects, barely more than the shadows they cast upon the desert—one and the same, every face a complete mystery.

Some of the houses were fortresses; a sizeable home in the center accompanied four towers in each corner connected by walls. I wondered as we passed why they needed such fortification. Children played in the fields close to the earthen ramparts under the careful eye of a mother resting in the shade. Under the palm tree, I caught her eye wandering from beneath her veil. She faltered in the attempt not to notice the invading army, gazing through us without discomfort or surprise. The M-88 passed through an underpass when word came over the speaker that a civilian was waving forward, as if warning us of something ahead. The menacing caravan of tanks kept cautious, but that anxiety soon elevated.

A call erupted from Captain Gunn notifying Hells Wrecker that an ammunition box was lying on the left side of the road. The captain's tank ahead had just passed the large wooden box; it was up to the M-88 to destroy it. Before entering Iraq, general instruction was given to destroy Iraqi munitions so they could not be utilized by the enemy. The commander of the M-88 traversed the M2 over the left side—the same machine gun that had been jamming when test fires were attempted. I lifted my eyebrows out of sight, knowing that it would simply jam again. I touched the M-16 rifle at my side, readying myself to perform the task that our unreliable, dirty main gun couldn't.

As soon as the captain breathed his order, shots rang out from the left. Rounds impacted Hells Wrecker all around me. The whiff each round made danced around my torso. Unaware that rounds had struck the metal near his head, the driver continued his straight course. An oil jug riddled with bullets spewed its hot contents onto the blacktop, spattering the hull. I bolted out of my hatch fully exposed. Muzzle directly in front of the driver's nose, I began firing at the innocent grass field making the attempt on our lives. The familiar jamming and cursing of the M-88 commander barely registered, my sole focus on the gentle sway of a green ocean. Nature was my foe, a shield to the heart that so coveted my demise. He was in there somewhere.

The familiar chugging of Hells Wrecker overcame my senses within seconds. Momentarily, there was peace. I hurriedly grabbed more ammunition inside, grazing by Willie dead asleep in his cap. Total concentration, which I had never experienced, glazed my eyes. Adrenaline pumped in my veins.

The convoy ahead staged tanks to the right and left side of the road, in the familiar herring-bone defensive formation that we were all accustomed to. We heard shots and numerous transmissions that the enemy was attacking with small arms fire from either side of the road. It was an ambush. The forward elements of the convoy, tanks, AAVs, then the M-88 stopped fully and engaged various targets utilizing "recon by fire." I fired at anything that looked suspicious. Shots continued from everywhere—from motionless tall grass and seemingly vacant mud-brick homes. It struck me then that nobody knew exactly what we were engaging. The homes became littered with machine gun fire. Pocks and wisps of smoke exploded from the ground, rounds accurate to the shooter's erratic aim. Marines cooped up in Kuwait for months now had the chance to unleash on a helpless machine-gun trigger. Though no guerilla was ever seen during this tremendous volley of retaliation, our minds became red with the yearning to destroy, partly to take back the pieces of our lives that we had thus far spent so miserably here.

"Move on! Move on!" our captain shouted. "Keep pressing forward!"

Tanks wheeled left and right, back into a neat column on the pavement. My eyes, just above the threshold of the hatch, rarely perceived the origin of the shots. Not soon after the first contact, where nerves remained tense, we received word that a white truck had been spotted coming in from the east. I squinted far off to the right, seeing men in black leaping from a pickup, diving into the concealing field. Fedayeen Saddam. A hundred yards out, the truck abruptly stopped. I lifted my rifle and took my best aim at the driver: a shot, then one to the passenger. I was an expert shot, and it filled me with adrenaline knowing they were dead. I felt as if would live forever.

Adrenaline

Forgive me but you have no idea where I have been.
Not just a time in place but a state of mind
Once I never thought death could touch me, I was in that place
For a moment
Yet it is that moment that dictates my passion in everything I do
I also know how close death is, I have seen it and it has not yet taken me
So, forgive me my passions
For I have been at ends of a spectrum you cannot understand.

The convoy pressed on. Thoughts rushed into my mind as a short period of peace ensued. For the first time in my life, I had killed. Other Marines on the front no doubt were thinking the same thing.

Fields of tall grass like cattails were everywhere. The enemy had to be in there, and what a handsome convoy we made, moving thirty miles an hour—a prize at the cost of a rocket. These tanks had the best armor in the world but remained inferior to an innocent field where the enemy could shoot at our rear.

Not a half mile from the first incident, Iron Horse slowed to a stop once again, the lead tank's .50 caliber bursting out in the direction of yet another volley of incoming fire. In the midst of the crossfire ahead, infantry spilled from one of the AAVs, sprinting to a small ridge to the right. Captain Gunn had made the obvious decision to hold ground until the threat was extinguished. One of the lead tanks rolled in close to where they were posted, assisting the men with larger caliber fire.

There were homes, a large one in particular on the left side of the highway. Not a soul was visible. Five were on the right, equally motionless in the chaos of destruction. The infantry set up facing the five, around fifty yards from the closest ones. Picking up binoculars, I gazed to the homes and fields quickly. Complete stillness. The occasional pop ruptured my ears. I spotted a building with a clothesline attached to it in the distance. There he was. Five soldiers ran toward the clothesline. All had matching clothes of solid black; all five were carrying rocket-propelled grenades.

Dropping the binoculars, I flicked the communication switch. "Over there! They're carrying RPGs!" The Hercules commander wheeled, this time with his rifle aimed in at the five jogging toward the building away from us. Doing the same, I opened up on them; one arched and crashed to the earth, rocket launcher tumbling across the ground. His brethren, leaving him for dead, sprinted into the building.

Then chaos broke loose. Civilians crowded into the areas we were engaging, mixing in with the enemy. Guerillas ran to and fro in the distance, perhaps mingling with their own families. The Fedayeen had done something. They must have threatened the civilians out of their homes. I spotted a pink shawl on a small girl, running, arms outstretched, into a mother crouched beside one of the heated buildings. An old man standing beside a wooden light pole dashed aside as a bullet splintered it next to him. People sprinted between homes, a mother hastily rounding up her children, a man dressed in white diving to the dirt, all in the midst of the true enemy, cunning in his methods of camouflage. The civilians haphazardly made their way to the fields far from the battle and back into their homes, hiding. An explosion vomited rock and shrapnel close to the infantry; RPGs sliced the air in every direction. Then I heard it. An unknown voice over the radio shouted in my ear.

"Shoot everything that moves! SHOOT EVERYTHING THAT MOVES!"

I felt the hot buttstock of the rifle against my cheek and took aim at the crowd 300 yards away. I adjusted my rear sight to match. I was a rifleman, and I was not going to miss. Conscience. My conscience was blotted out; my eyes became fixed on the targets. I wanted them to die. And as if I were outside my body looking inward, I fired. Again and again. Screaming. My conscience was screaming to stop because

I did not know for sure who I was engaging. They were wearing white and racing in between the homes; the Fedayeen were wearing black. I just saw them and then they disappeared. I was firing at civilians! My hands froze. I lowered my rifle.

Aaron. What did you do?

Rounds continued to flare from the houses and fields distant. Two rockets cut the air directly for Hells Wrecker, stopped short, and exploded a hundred feet from impact, dirt, sand, and shrapnel flying everywhere. The explosions, attempts at my life as well as those around, did not register. Gaping at the settling dirt, I felt as if I had been lulled into a dream, not caring about the noise, the hearty shouts of Marines, not giving heed that there might be more rockets aimed directly for me. Focus determined reality. My attention diverted to the single tank off to the right that had been supporting the infantry. The menacing turret slowly fixed its sight on the closest mud house and fired. A deafening blast followed the tire-sized hole it ripped. Like a needle through a sheet of paper, clean and swift, another and another was fired until the home collapsed in a cloud of dust.

Emptiness. I remember the emptiness inside of me, a void where memory should be. I lost focus as my reactions to the gunfire outside the M-88 softened. Sounds faded to whispers, and for a short time I remained in a world of no thought, word, or question. Complete nothingness.

Miscommunication made its way through the confused Marines:

"The building with the flag leaning up against it! Over to the right! See it?"

The firing tank responded, "I see the building you described; over. But cannot find the black flag on its side; over." A shot.

"NEGATIVE! The building to the right! What are you firing at!?"

Despite the effort expended to determine which building held the Fedayeen, every home in the area received the same treatment—shot through with a tank round. All of them. Mud homes that appeared to have no role whatsoever in the tirade were pounded as fiercely as the next. Heaven only knew what was in those buildings. We heard rumors that infantry later charged in to discover old men and their families hiding under beds and in basements. Under the debris were also the combatants who, under the charge of Fedayeen, had passports from far away as Egypt and Yemen, and as close as Iran and Syria.

The area settled in smoke and all was quiet once again. I lifted my hands in front of my face, studying the wrinkles and orange dirt upon them. I will never forget my hands. They had just killed. Not in defense, or in protection of what I held most dear, but in necessity rooted in an others' ambition. I had become an instrument of war. All acts became justified hiding behind the command of the unknown voice. Did this absolve me from sin? In my heart I knew it didn't. My heart was sick, my morals were struck, my soul tainted: I would never know if, or how many, civilians died that day.

God weighs the soul in eternity.

CHAPTER V

The Nature of Our War

We have learned, to our regret, that while you are certainly better for preparing, the war you prepare for is rarely the war you get.

GENERAL VICTOR KRULAK, USMC

I LONGED FOR THE woods. Those silent trails where all you heard was music of birds. There were few birds in Iraq, and I had not paused long enough to hear their song. Peace, precious peace. All I wanted was to return to the time I had peace before combat, and to sit. To just be alone. Everything had changed. Was this the warfare that my superiors didn't talk about? I think it was. Our preparation wasn't enough. I hated the Marines and being around them. I hated myself. So, for the next few days I excluded myself from everything I could. I did not play cards, I didn't laugh, and I didn't socialize. Pigeon keeping me company, I wrote fervently; I was blessed and cursed with time.

I began to think about the nature of Operation Iraqi Freedom. I sat there, far north of the buildings and lives we just wrecked, and ruminated about the purpose of this war. I should have had the presence of mind to question it further than I did, giving myself up as someone else's man, a pawn for the sake of patriotism. It wasn't that simple, though; I needed to understand the war. It was unfolding differently than I had been trained.

Since landing in Kuwait, we had prepared for a conventional war against conventional forces, but to my alarm we were fighting unconventional forces, fanatics both foreign and domestic, hiding behind civilians bent on destroying as many Americans that they could. This war was not solitary in nature. It was deeper than simply invading Iraq. Fueling the fury was a deep-seated resentment for America and what she stood for. I had never imagined such a thing as fanatics fighting for a mass murderer, dying for Saddam and not for anything else. It was madness.

The truth about Operation Iraqi Freedom was that, for sporadic moments at least, we waged total war. It was opposite the doctrine of limited war that the United States was used to. The scathing truth remains clear—at least 124,000 Iraqi civilians were killed in the war and occupation. Some estimates top a million. They were the afterbirth of an otherwise clean and efficient war that ate up the newspapers back home and fueled the anti-war protests around the globe. The simple fact was that sometimes we cast away the morals and high ethical standards of the United States armed services to achieve our goal, and that was to subjugate Iraq and kill Saddam Hussein. Anyone who got in the way was of secondary importance. The order "recon by fire" was the single order that sacked Iraq. General Tommy Franks was quoted saying, "We don't do body counts" to the *San Francisco Chronicle* in May 2003, and at the time that was a correct appraisal. And what did we get from all this? The most efficient invasion in history.

How many stories, I wondered after the war, can be told of how a soldier mistakenly killed a civilian as a result of combat action, or purposely killed one to accomplish the mission? *Countless,* I told myself. Though I could never interview enough soldiers and Marines to establish the fact, I knew it to be true by the numbers. It was total warfare the guerilla wanted, and we obliged with devastating effect.

They tried to teach morals in the Marine Corps in the hope that some of it would stick when the time came. It did for me, and I struggle with it every day; I know my comrades do as well, because they know what really happened on the ground in Iraq and keep those truths locked up, seldom revealed. It was the price of accomplishing the mission, which was commonly to root out the combatants from the civilians at any given time. The Iraqi combatant who disguised himself in the civilian population received the most contempt from US forces. How dare the guerilla attack us from within his loved ones' reach. He pushed us to the extreme, he pushed us to kill, and doing so destroyed our sense of morality honorably won as fighting men. Mission accomplished, you bastards.

In total war, moral injury strikes everyone. Morals are hard won in life, and you have them if you don't shed innocent blood, if you are not the "bad guy." You believe that you are a good American soldier as long as you do what is right—what is chivalrous. American soldiers have been reared to embody the best qualities admired by a peaceable society. A culture that values a good fight so long as it can be stopped at the bell. A culture that doesn't understand total war; one that frowns on its ugliness, and which hangs up its fighting men, knowing nothing of military matters. The reality of war is something modern society wants kept in the dark. And most of the time, it remains unseen.

But what of the men? Soldiers regret things that they have done to bring war to the enemy; the most effective way to kill a cause, kill their motivation, is to submit them to your will. Destroying homes, destroying the means by which to thrive, bringing the war into the hearts of civilians, was precisely what our enemy was doing. He was exposing a weakness—or so he thought—in the American military; he assumed that we would not act if civilians were mixed into the fray. In truth, it was his best chance of succeeding against the technologically and numerically superior force. Fear. He exposed fear because he knew we were trained to "do the right thing" in the face of adversity. He wanted war with America, not war *for* Saddam, and that made it a more personal matter. Our reaction to the guerilla reflected his success, as it did our seriousness. Total war does not sit well with good men. I had to go deeper.

★ ★ ★ ★ ★

We were fighting a war on the run. Sprinting to Baghdad was our priority, which meant not entangling ourselves in firefights along the way. Speed and time had removed us from fighting a war of convention much as our enemy utilized civilians to avoid fighting a war of convention. If we stopped for every firefight along the way, our enemy would regroup and become stronger. The result was two opposing forces slammed together with shock and awe, ready to do battle and forced into it. It was a highway war. The tempo of battle was just too fast to fight a limited war governed by the rules of engagement. Reconnaissance, foresight into enemy territory, was nonexistent. We resorted to fire, and that in turn resulted in fire. The enemy was made more numerous when the civilian picked up his AK-47 to defend his home. We made the enemy more numerous using "recon by fire," but at the same time that method so shocked the enemy that he hid however he could to keep fighting. There was little else he could do to be effective against the highway-bound force. Civilians were the true victims. This was total war.

The average soldier was in the dark. He was isolated with his unit in the back of an amtrack, or a Bradley, or a seven-ton truck or a Humvee. They had little knowledge outside what they were doing at the moment. I felt for these men. They had radio to keep abreast of the movements of their units, but they seldom had knowledge of the grand movements of the army and what the objectives were outside their direct control. If they got wind of their coordinates, it was moot within hours, the Marines moving so fast that one could be in desert or a jungle at the drop of a dime. When the door of the AAV came crashing down, the Marines had to think fast and gain knowledge of the tactical situation within seconds. The best leader was one who could digest the situation and direct his Marines appropriately for success. After combat, that precious moment when the Marines grasped their surroundings, they filed into the AAVs once again on the road to another firefight. The walls of the amtrack were suffocating, the Marines standing on their seats to see outside. Those who sat or dozed as the convoy pressed on were truly in the dark.

Our armies were beholden to their convoys. If we had a weakness, that was it. The Marines were bound to the highway. If the enemy had the good sense to resist us, then he should have been constantly regrouping north, staging the strongest fighters in the Karbala Gap where the US forces must pass through to get to Baghdad. We moved slowly as a mechanized force due to the vast difference between the tanks in front and the rear-most guard. Sometimes a convoy spanned 100 kilometers from front to rear. It was the Marines who were primarily highway-bound, whereas the Army, approaching from the desert to the left flank, was more fluid, mobile, separate from the highways. The Army had the luxury of attacking and shifting location as needed to engage Saddam's token force where it hid in waiting.

The US airborne and special force troops landing north near Mosul and Kirkuk were a shock force meant to reinforce the 70,000 Kurdish Peshmerga fighting against Saddam and take out the heavier concentration of tanks and mechanized forces there. More paratroopers landed in the far west near Ar-Rutbah, and they were the least mobile, isolated in the desert. They, and the Army to the west, had more tactical freedom than the Marines.

The Marines were poised to take the brunt of the fighting, which we did. RCT-5 encountered more resistance and combat than any other combat team. The tanks' proximity to their respective convoys limited their combat capability to within a dozen miles from support. The curse of heavy tanks was their reliance on fuel and supply. But this did not satisfy me; I had to question the war itself. Was our war a just war? I had questioned it before combat, but after combat, that question changed me. It changed everything. I now viewed the war with an unobstructed lens, as one who was there and fired the bullets and scattered the enemy. As one who was there when the civilians hid for their lives, and as one who sacked the oil fields and took prisoners. A just war was what I needed to ease my soul—a war founded on rights worthy of sacrifice.

I had read Carl Von Clausewitz and Baron Antoine de Jomini, great philosophers of war, and concluded they were the compass through which I needed to examine this struggle. Jomini, the best lens in which to examine mechanized warfare, states,

> The most just war is one which is founded upon undoubted rights, and which, in addition, promises to the state advantages commensurate with the sacrifices required and the hazards incurred. Unfortunately, in our times there are so many doubtful and contested rights that most wars, though apparently based upon bequests, or wills, or marriages, are in reality but wars of expediency.[74]

Was it a just war? Undoubted rights of humanity are life, liberty, and the pursuit of happiness.[75] From the humble outlook of the Declaration of Independence, Thomas Jefferson, as John Locke before him, was correct. The Iraqis deserved the same human rights, and that was just. The Constitution was worth fighting for, and it was an attack on the Constitution on September 11 that I was in the desert fighting. The attack was a threat against my way of life, and that was worth fighting for. But there was something else. We sought Al-

---
74   Baron De Jomini, *The Art of War*, translated by Captain G. H. Mendell, and Lieutenant W. P. Craighill, 2011: Bottom of the Hill Publishing.
75   Fundamentals in the United States Declaration of Independence derived originally from John Locke.

Qaeda and claimed that Saddam had provided them nourishment. We sought to avenge ourselves for 3,000 lives lost on our soil against a predator whose allegiance knew no bounds but contempt for the United States. We were attacking Iraq, a nation that had no direct role in September 11. Osama Bin Laden had been a wealthy Saudi. According to our leadership, the people had been oppressed since Saddam came to power in 1979, and they needed US intervention.

So, that was it. I was making war in Iraq not for the Constitution but for human rights, freedom from tyranny, the causes the United States had championed against Britain. I understood it, but nowhere in our Constitution does it obligate us to overthrow regimes for the sake of humanity, and since I fought for the Constitution, I felt misplaced, inappropriate, unjust. We forced freedom on a people that had not yet risen up to claim it themselves; the Iraqi people were not ready. They did not want a democracy. It was not our business to dictate the next course of development for an entire nation, and in that we were unjust.

Would this war provide the United States "advantages commensurate with the sacrifices required"? The United States could only afford as many casualties as its citizens would permit. The Vietnam War was proof of this logic. So, it was to be a quick war or a failure. Many view Operation Enduring Freedom as a failure in proportion with the lives lost. The advantage of this war, according to the Bush Administration, was one less nation that harbored terrorists, but in truth any nation can harbor a terrorist as long as that terrorist is acting in the interest of the state. It is not reasonable to make war on all nations that harbor your enemy, and according to the Bush Doctrine, that was what needed to be done. The doctrine is impossible.

There was nothing but rhetoric from the Bush administration explaining that Saddam had terrorists that were acting against the United States; there was no proof. Al-Qaeda was everywhere. It is possible they were in Iraq, but they were mostly concentrated in

Afghanistan, Syria, and Somalia. If we were interested in wiping out the Al-Qaeda who attacked the US on 9/11, there were other nations worthier of assault than Iraq, such as Afghanistan, where we were fighting the Al-Qaeda daily in pursuance of a perverted doctrine. Even the oil we captured would not be ours; it belonged to Iraq, and Iraq later cost the US taxpayers billions in reconstruction and aid just to keep it afloat. The United States would sacrifice much in war—worst of all, 4,491 US soldiers dead and many more casualties—just to have another friendly government in the Middle East. The advantages were not commensurate with the sacrifices required, and that was unjust.

What about weapons of mass destruction? Is it a right of the state to have WMD? If it is a right of the state regardless of who or what controls the state, then going to war to take away WMD from Saddam was unjust. Here are some universal truths:

1) It is the right of every nation to have weapons to defend itself. That is without question.
2) It is the right of every nation to go to war if it so chooses. That is without question. "War is merely a continuation of policy by other means," according to Clausewitz, and since every nation may make policy, they may go to war.[76]
3) It is therefore the right of every nation to have weapons capable of destroying an enemy.
4) Saddam was a ruthless killer using WMD on his own people and against Iran with devastating effect: that is without question.

He used weapons that caused death much as a conventional bullet would. The difference was in the interest of humanity—not nations. A nation does not have the right to possess WMD if they have been used on noncombatants, or to use them without restraint. Saddam violated both tenets, according to the UN, giving the US

---

76 Carl Von Clausewitz, *On War*, Edited by Michael Howard, and Peter Paret, 1984: Princeton University Press, 87

justification to dethrone the dictator and seize the country and its oil assets. But what if, as Saddam claimed, he did not have WMD? What if UN inspectors never found any because they did not exist? A high-ranking defector of the regime, Hussein Kamel al-Majid, stated years before OIF that all WMD material was destroyed. If he was compliant with the UN and he had no WMD left, then going to war with Saddam because of WMD was unjustified. No WMD was ever found in Iraq after 2003; therefore, unless it happens to be found hidden away in the future, the United States was unjustified in invading Iraq on that premise.

It was a war of expediency, then. A matter of policy. In 1998, President Bill Clinton was approached by Donald Rumsfeld and Paul Wolfowitz about invading Iraq. It was unfinished business since the Gulf War; these policymakers believed that Iraq had to go and a pro-Western government installed in its place. The American people would not have stood for a ground war at the time, but bombing was almost always acceptable, and that was exactly what President Clinton did, initiating Operation Desert Fox, where the US and British bombed Iraqi chemical weapons facilities because they had not been complying with UN inspectors. Clinton also signed into law HR 4655, the Iraqi Liberation Act, funding opposition groups to oust the regime and replace it with a democracy.

Taking out Saddam was not a new idea. Saddam was an upstart firing scuds at his neighbors, including Israel. There had been whispers in the US government about taking Iraq all along. The United States could use another ally in the Middle East like Israel, but, unlike Israel, Iraq had oil and was centrally located, giving the US more power over other Middle Eastern states. It was expedient, useful, and convenient to establish a pro-US government in Iraq.

We were justified invading Iraq because of humanity—not oil. Jomini states,

> A war of invasion without good reason—like that of Genghis Khan—is a crime against humanity; but it may be excused, if not approved, when induced by great interests or when conducted with good motives.[77]

Saddam murdered about a million people during his reign. Saddam had proven himself a ruthless killer. That was without question. His crimes against humanity were without question. So, why would people fight for him? I fought to defend the Constitution of the United States from enemies foreign and domestic. It was from that oath *and* humanity that I justified going to war. The attack on our soil September 11, 2001, was enough reason for me. But what justified my enemy? Did he honestly believe that life under a tyrant was worth fighting for?

The bullets whizzing by my head were proof *something* was worth fighting for. There was some principle that lay just under the surface.

Most were afraid. They were scared to death of Saddam and his henchmen. It is well known that the Ba'ath militia and Fedayeen Saddam threatened death to civilians who did not fight or killed those who resisted the regime. That was only half the reason. The other half was simple. Fanatics who entered Iraq to fight from all corners of the world did so because they hated the United States, hated the West, what it stood for, and its interference in Middle-Eastern affairs. That was the principle. That was worth dying for. Not Saddam.

Outside the benefit to humanity, then, our war was unjust. That did not sit well with me. I focused on the benefit to the Iraqis. *They* were the prize, and not the killing of a few Fedayeen. Killing was a pure luxury on the road to Baghdad. Yes, it was a jewel on one's crown to know that evil men were destroyed, but at the same time it

---

77   Baron De Jomini, *The Art of War,* translated by Captain G. H. Mendell, and Lieutenant W. P. Craighill, 2011: Bottom of the Hill Publishing, 12.

was an unwelcome one. It changed me, and I hated how the nature of the killing caused me moral injury because civilians were mixed in the fray. The only thing that truly ails a soldier is the regret for things he has done. I had that regret, and it would shape how I interacted with the world, with every soul, for the rest of my life.

In war, truth is the first casualty.
AESCHYLUS

CHAPTER VI

THE CLOVERLEAF AND THE NIGHT OF MORTARS

The greatest cohesion is found in the smallest units.
THE MARINE CORPS INSTITUTE, LEADERSHIP CREDO

MARCH 27 WAS A hellish day for our entire company. Bravo was ordered to seize Han'tush Airfield north of Ad Diwaniyah to allow our C-130s to land and resupply with desperately needed provisions. Along Highway 1 the company encountered successive ambushes with small arms and RPGs. Nowhere was safe. We rolled north and obliterated countless sand-bagged bunkers along the road. They were everywhere, sometimes occupied and sometimes not. I saw bodies on the side of the road; one was sawed in half. The overpasses were dangerous as well. Gutsy Fedayeen, Ba'ath militia, and foreign fighters would fire from beneath the overpasses at tankers. It was as if they were taking siestas in the bridges' shade and suddenly roused to American tanks zooming past them. Most of them got off a few potshots and scattered until they gave up or were killed. We learned to hate overpasses.

The lead vehicle received a direct impact from an RPG but kept going; the engineer platoon in the rear also received RPG fire, resulting in a Marine killed and another wounded—the first from our convoy since the beginning of the war. Air support was called in. A-10 "Warthogs" with their giant 30 mm rotary cannon swept the area, firing 1,800 rounds a minute at three M-80s and at least one BMP. Two F-18s came in and dropped ordinance as well. Apache Cobras weaved the skies above dismounted infantry and made quick work of them. They sought out the enemy around the highway for miles as the tanks serviced several bunkers on the strip. Sitting in the front seat of the M-88 just behind the tanks, the scene was full of ricochets, the deafening bang of ordinance, and fire from red-hot metal. The Iraqis were taken completely by surprise.

The Wolfpack, 3rd LAR, fast becoming legendary, led the attack at the airstrip. Leading RCT-5, the company spotted and obliterated twelve Iraqi AAA teams and took a dozen EPWs (enemy prisoners of war).[78] They scouted the area and found two Al Samoud surface-to-surface missiles not far from the airstrip, significant because they were outlawed by UN resolutions. Saddam obviously was not above hiding contraband. No sooner was the airfield surrounded by RCT-5 than a C-130 that had been circling overhead roared over Hells Wrecker and touched down on the dirt runway. It motivated the hell out of me. The airfield was a wide road defended by a company-sized force who barely put up a fight. Helicopters also touched down, and I saw our wounded and honored dead loaded upon them with a trail of medics.

Only God knew if our wounded from the engineer platoon would survive. The war became more real to me after seeing the

---

78 Groen, Michael, *With the 1st Marine Division in Iraq*, accessed October 12, 2015, http://www.marines.mil/Portals/59/Publications/With%20the%201st%20 Marine%20Division%20in%20Iraq,%202003%20%20PCN%2010600000000_18.pdf

gurneys; up to this point we'd had a field day invading Iraq with no casualties. If seeing our fallen did not phase the Marines, the events of March 27 sobered everyone. For the time being, the C-130 meant we could keep going. It meant desperately needed parts for our rolling stock, from Hummers to heavy tanks; it meant oil, food, and, most importantly for us, it meant mail. The tanks left within minutes of securing Han'tush, unable to enjoy the victory, and before we knew it we were on the highway once again.

Leaving Han'tush behind, many of us asked the obvious—*Where is Saddam's air force?* Since heavy tanks were the spear tip into Iraq, tankers often worried about their potential worst enemy—air attacks, especially from helicopters. Though by 2003 Iraq's air defense force had increased to 17,000 men from 10,000 a decade earlier, it was incredibly weakened by US enforcement of the no-fly zones.[79] Four thousand strike and support "sorties" in Iraq's no-fly zones were made from March first through the twentieth alone.[80]

A modern mechanized army requires the oversight of a modern air force, and Iraq had none. At the close of the Gulf War in 1991, when the humiliated Iraqi Army retreated from Kuwait to the safety of its interior, the Iraqi military establishment had suffered a deathblow that would return to haunt it. After the war, there was no significant effort to rebuild the Iraqi air defense systems destroyed by the US Air Force. In the words of an Iraqi general, talk of the reestablishment of air defense from 1991 on was "lies, all lies."[81] Throughout the invasion, no Marine I knew ever saw enemy aircraft.

The greatest enemy to the Americans might have been the 513 combat aircraft and 160 armed helicopters the Iraqi Army possessed at the time of the invasion.[82] Helicopters are tank killers, and Iraq might have been able to utilize them had they not buried them—

---

79 Cordesman, *The Military Balance*, 303.
80 Hosmer, *Iraqi Resistance*, 75.
81 William Branigin, "A Brief, Bitter War for Iraq's Military Officers," The *Washington Post*, April 27, 2003, p. A25.
82 Cordesman, *The Military Balance*, 303.

literally. The coalition airstrikes before the war not only caused morale to drop but also generated an order for all combat aircraft to be disassembled and buried in the desert.[83] The logic was sound. In order to preserve the asset from destruction, it had to be hidden from the view of US bombers. By consequence, Iraqi aircraft were completely grounded when the invasion began taking the Iraqi Air Force out of the equation. They probably would not have been very effective, anyway. The weapon systems were at least fifteen years old and lacked replacement parts for reasons already mentioned, and the Iraqi Air Force was obliged to maintain twelve types of them.[84] With the vast array of aged weapon systems to coordinate, it was not likely that the Iraqis could have stopped many US tanks given their condition. An Iraqi commander of air defense said, "[M]y own ground-to-air missiles had a range of only 43 kilometers . . . their planes could detect our radar and fly faster than my missiles and then turn around and bomb my crews. So, I would send only one battery to engage an American aircraft and [kept] the rest safe."[85]

Racing Highway 1, repeatedly under fire, was getting old. We fired at so many suspicious targets that they blurred into one great violation of the rules of engagement. RCT-5 got too far ahead of the rest of the coalition and was ordered to pull back by CENTCOM (United States Central Command) and General Mattis. We could have sacked Baghdad all by ourselves within five days, I surmised, but the glory would have to be shared. Only four and a half days after D-Day RCT-5, and RCT-7 behind it, we were at a crossroads. We called it the "cloverleaf" in reference to what it looked like from the air. Ad Diwaniyah was to the west and Afak to the east. We spent the greater part of three days rolling north under fire to where Highway 1 split into two other roads. We returned to the cloverleaf primarily

---

83 Cordesman, *The Military Balance*, 298.
84 Ibid., 296.
85 Robert Fisk, "Ruling the Airways: How America Demoralized the Iraqi Army," *The Independent*, May 24, 2003, http://web.lexis-nexis.com/universe/document?_m=d94acd59d2a42e30ab941b70369be73.

at night. It was sort of a resting place where we waited for RCT-1 to catch up and for the Army to finish up its mission to isolate As Samwah and An Najaf, which they accomplished by March 28. The enemy took advantage of our predictability. And to top things off, Willie the pigeon had disappeared.

★ ★ ★ ★

"Corporal Grant, get up! It's your turn for watch." The familiar red lens flashlight pierced the dark interior of Hells Wrecker.

"Shit!" I said aloud. Time for two hours of fire-watch.

The midnight air was as crisp and cool as it could be at the cloverleaf. Peeling off my sleeping bag, cold tremors swept through me as I slipped my boots on. The snoring Marines inside didn't make the slightest movement at my commotion. I stood up on the M-88 and took time to give the stars attention. The constellation Orion had always been with me when all felt foreign. I managed a smile. The ground was soft, almost moist between my destination and the M-88. By the time my duty expired, it would undoubtedly be as slick as a bog.

Being a mechanic, I had no idea how to effectively fire a 120 mm main gun. So, there were two of us, Corporal Heffner and myself, both there to make sure one another remained conscious. It was helpful. Between the times when Heffner scanned the area for hostiles, we spoke of home. Since we were both from New York, it was nothing to make two hours pass easily. We equally missed New York, our families, the changing of the seasons, even the winter.

"Almost 2 a.m.," I said. "I'm going to wake up our oncoming duty." I reached up, pulling my body out of the turret, when a sound overcame my senses—whistling. Upper body out of the hatch, I peered into the darkness, the sound emanating from directly above. "What the—"

As soon as I opened my mouth, a blast issued from directly in front of the tank. Chunks of earth slammed against my body, accompanied with a fierce wind of shrapnel clanking all around me.

Bashing my head against the hatch, I slid back down into the turret. Another blast ensued, showering pieces of dirt into the opening.

"Are you okay? Are you okay?" Heffner cried. I nodded just as Captain Gunn rolled over in his sleeping bag on top of the turret, grabbed the radio, and began shouting orders. Thud after thud echoed in the night; tanks came alive searching for the cunning enemy.

"I've got to get to the Hercules!" I shouted.

"Oh no, no, NO!" he shouted back. "You stay in here!" I tried to get up, but he clasped my jacket with his left hand and hammered on his gunner's controls with his right. "STAY DOWN!"

He only kept me a few seconds, but it was long enough for half a dozen mortar blasts to dance around outside. Hoisting my body out of the hatch once again, I escaped Heffner's grip and brushed shoulders with the captain as he leapt into my seat. From the top of the M1-A1 turret to the ground was about eight feet, a fact that didn't frighten me as much as a shrapnel wound; so I jumped. After the weightlessness, my feet caught the slippery mud, my toes shot out behind me, and I landed stomach down in the muck. Another fantastic thud ripped the earth nearby as I lay facedown next to the captain's tank. There was no pain, at least not at the time, but I lay there disoriented, trying to breathe, benefiting from my training to stay low.

My helmet dug into the earth as I scraped my way forward, low-crawling with my rifle in hand. I thought of my training. Boot camp, Parris Island, South Carolina, where I had drilled like this over and again. There, I had crawled under barbed wire an absolute mess, but I didn't care. I did exactly as the drill instructors said as the machine gun fire echoed across the field of suffering recruits. I knew men had been killed on the field in training, and I was not about to be one of them. The drill instructor shouted, and on cue I flipped over on my back, rifle on my chest, and pushed my way forward with my legs trembling. I was exhausted, but I did as I was told under that razor-sharp wire, crawling through the mud puddles where only my lips were above the water, and I was thankful for each breath when I could get it.

My mind drifted to another boot camp incident while chunks of earth and shrapnel flew around me for what seemed like an eternity. I remember looking at a fellow recruit crying as he tried to do his push-ups. The night before, I told him, "We are in God's hand, brother, not in theirs." He had been placed at the front of the groaning platoon to be made an example of. The mistake he made escaped me. I just remembered four screaming drill instructors around him calling him names and insulting everything he was. What could he do but break down? He was crying; the first recruit I had seen do so. I don't think I had ever seen someone so alone. I knew if I were in his shoes, I would have needed help. To that point, I prided myself on lying so low that the instructors barely knew my name; it was safer that way.

Closing my eyes, I searched for strength, finding my sluggard muscle renewed. Shooting up from the push-up position, I sprinted to where my fellow recruit stood paralyzed in fear. Inserting myself in front of the screaming sergeant I told him, "Show them what a man you are!" immediately pulling him down by the sleeve into position and doing push-ups with him face-to-face. The yelling drowned in a muted echo, and the recruit's red eyes lost the humiliation that froze him. He succeeded.

Afterward, the nerves took hold. When ordered back to our bunks, my knees shook. Only moments before, I had left the drill instructors speechless. Then, realizing what was owed, I knelt beside my bed and thanked God for the strength He had given me to make a difference. I dismissed weakness in that pain, and welcomed a man I barely recognized, who was more like myself.

After my prayer, our senior drill instructor ordered me to his office and said as I stood there at attention, "I wish I could put your heart into all the other recruits here."

Those memories were gone as soon as they came, and I lay there under fire contemplating. I could have low-crawled to the M-88, or I could have run, perhaps saving lives by getting to Hells Wrecker in time to muster the crew for combat. It was selfish to think I could allow a mortar or the enemy to take out Hells Wrecker with me a hundred yards off, facedown in the muck.

Courage was sapped by my desire to stay low, to stay safe. Fear paralyzed my bones like being naked before God. Here in this moment was a new chapter, another instance where I had to dismiss fear and be reborn. It was an initiation; I braved the field. Birth. A baptism by fire. Like being saved at age thirteen, the intense fear I felt before the pivotal moment of absolute freedom in God. I was free. Calm, facing my death in a muddy waste in Iraq. Yes. It was time to move.

In a pause in the chaos, I scurried from a prone position to a sprint where oxygen empowered me to reach the M-88 a hundred yards away. Time slowed. Every step I took the mortars followed with earth and metal. Every step was a miracle. A mortar sliced the air above my head with a whistle as I clambered inside. Methodically, I slammed the hatch above my seat and drew my pistol. The tiny, three-inch-thick windows of the Hercules yielded no sign of enemy movement. Indeed, as soon as I readied to start the sixty-ton hulk from a cold sleep, complete silence overcame the night.

I glanced from one periscope window to the next instinctively like an animal; I remembered communications. I flicked on the radio, hearing corporals, lieutenants, and Captain Gunn drowning out each other, but I understood the message in seconds. We were to hold our position. It wasn't a simple matter to defend a position with an M-88 Hercules. All we had was an unclean, unreliable, fully exposed .50 caliber machine gun, four M16-A2 service rifles with approximately 120 rounds apiece, four AT-4 rocket launchers, and a handful of grenades. We were better off in a foxhole considering our size. And who knew what was out there, the tree line being so close. If the enemy landed so much as one rocket-propelled grenade on our hull, it would stun us long enough for them to come and finish the job.

The crew stubbornly refused to wake despite my commotion and nagging; after all the days we had been driving to Baghdad, I couldn't blame them. I spent the next hours pointing an M16 toward the palm trees, waiting, my silhouette overexposed under the moonlight. God was good to me, I later reflected. He was in the night. He directed the shrapnel. There could be no other reason I didn't suffer a scratch, and the mortars never came again.

I reflected under the stars that few on earth experienced birth more than once. Forgotten was the moment we opened our eyes to the world, but what about those moments we remembered? Dismissing fear, I was reborn in front of a red-faced preacher as I sat there crying. I had never known that I never knew God until that moment. Thirteen years of saying I knew dashed aside in the moment that changed my life. There I was. Imperfect and trembling before God. I was reborn.

In Parris Island, I sat in a barber's chair and looked into the mirror. That was it. My birth into the Corps. The razor ground my scalp, releasing blood, and my lip trembled; drill instructors screaming, my eyes were wide with fear, locked in a body that did not dare show weakness. I looked small. Pathetic. That night, when all were in unsecure beds, recruits cried themselves to sleep, terrified eighteen-year-olds at the height of insecurity. I lay with a knot in my throat. The drill instructors were not gods, and for three months afflicted by them, I endured until the end. I was fearless when handed the Eagle, Globe, and Anchor. I was reborn a Marine, and nothing could stop me.

Fear and rebirth. Seeing the light cannot be taken; it cannot be replaced. It cannot be faked, it cannot be forgotten; and it cannot fail. Calm and focused, I breathed new air each time, as I did now. Renewed by the absence of trembling, I reflected under a slice of moon. I had no fear anymore. I was completely free.

★ ★ ★ ★

The next morning when Marines roused sluggishly from the night of mortars, we all had the obvious question in mind. According to what intelligence had been gathered, a small group of troops set up five mortar-launching devices close to a patch of woods nearby, quickly and skillfully under the cover of darkness. They fired a dozen rounds, packed up, and fled into the darkness. They were most likely Fedayeen.

I was so tired. I was definitely "in the zone," as the Marines would say, running mostly on adrenaline; my mind could not keep up. They say that a soldier can survive nonstop combat for seventy-two hours before fatigue affects motor skills and judgement. I was barely conscious. I knew I was less than mission capable. Nights advancing north with the constant threat of something happening to us barely kept me awake. They were pushing us to the limits of human endurance, and CENTCOM expected our fatigue. They should have issued us caffeine pills. Mothers of America probably would have protested, but it would have kept men alive. Sleep would save lives. How could we achieve true sleep? Personally, I could not because something always happened when I slept. I felt during the war I could not truly sleep until the job was done. "There's plenty of sleep when you're taking your dirt nap," my aunt would say, and I believed her. I had to survive. There were greater things for me in the future and I felt it in my bones.

The next day, while on a run with the tanks rolling north on Highway 1, we were ordered to literally plow over a mud-brick structure that possibly harbored the enemy. We had been receiving fire like usual, and our captain guessed at the origin of the shots. We rolled up to the square home standing about twelve feet tall and twenty feet square with palm leaves for a roof. I leapt out of my hatch, boots penetrating the sand below Hells Wrecker. I told the crew that we should not dare push it over until the interior had been scouted for anyone hiding inside.

As the afternoon sun pounded my helmet, I stepped forward, rifle pointing straight ahead, grazing the outer wall. Flies swarmed around my face, trying to get a taste of the sweat dripping off my nose. My thoughts drifted to something my aunt told me before I left for Kuwait: "NO HEROICS," and "DON'T VOLUNTEER FOR ANYTHING!" I missed her, and I knew every day my life was endangered—and not just because I volunteered to clear a building.

Automatic weapons fired in the distance. I couldn't bear the thought of crushing an innocent or allowing an explosion or attack to kill us. *What could be in this small home?* I was about to find out. Gliding along the mud wall tactically, the door was upon me.

"Dammit!" I cursed at myself. "Why don't you have backup?"

I stepped along a smooth pathway beyond the doorless entrance. It broke off to the right and left immediately. I jerked to the right, and then spun around to look behind. *Clear.* Any soul in the building would have heard the thumping of my heart in that moment. The end of Corporal Aaron Grant could have easily been dealt with a swift bullet to the back. I took every minute sound as a hostile action. I glided to the left side corridor and around, entering a single large chamber. I lowered my weapon. Nothing could have prepared me for the immediate sight within.

Wisps of blue, purple, and gold bedecked the smooth earthen walls. The border of its light was endless. Outlined in red, letters of black and faded blue, the Arabic script circled the entire room with elegant ease. My rifle left my grasp and dangled by the sling at my fingertips.

The same script repeated itself into infinity, the walls telling the selfsame story as one spun in circles in the middle, never faltering its humble purpose. I didn't need to understand its meaning as I descended into another world from behind a cloud of judgment. Flowers of gold and red pierced the dim light accompanying the ancient script.

The floors were smooth concrete; the area was clean as if its occupants had just left. There was a feeling of happiness in the air, and I was saddened in the knowledge that it must be destroyed. I exited the structure and decided not to tell anyone of the interior. Uttering the memory of what I knew must be demolished was useless. It needed to be done.

Hells Wrecker pushed the building over with ease until we crowned the pile of rubble. My guilt was overwhelming. *Who am I? Who are we to crash here as a tidal wave thinking it is we who hold the best qualities and secrets of life? We impose our culture onto those who believe in something so deeply few could fathom.* The script must have been from the Qur'an. *Damn this war,* I thought. Damn the enemy for shooting at us from his own homes. It was his fault we had to go to such extremes.

* * * * *

It was March 29, and the highway north of the cloverleaf was reasonably clear of enemy activity. Homes that were not pushed over were shot through with tank rounds; whatever was suspicious received recon by fire. I surmised that if an Iraqi was neutral before our activity north of the cloverleaf, then he became our enemy when he came home to see his home destroyed. At the end of the day, the guerillas won when we engaged them on their territory, recruiting untold numbers when we sought them out in the only way we knew how. The infantry behind the tanks spilled out with regularity, clearing buildings when ordered, but it was much easier and risked fewer Marines when we shot at the buildings instead. It was tried and tested, eliminating enemy fire without unnecessarily risking our own lives. If not for the fact that we were constantly under fire, it would have been shameful. This was total war. Damn the guerillas.

The days were not without definitive success though. Every weapon cache we discovered was a victory, and all around the cloverleaf there was many of them. The longer we stayed in the area, the more we discovered, and the more civilians helped us find them as well as the locations of the Fedayeen, Ba'ath militia, and foreign fighters. But it was a two-sided coin. The longer we stayed, the more aggravated our enemy became and the more of them poured out of the desert.

Emboldened Iraqis fought with more conviction, retaking the Han'tush airfield, but for just a few days. I saw it as an Iraqi victory, even if it was short lived. The Marines didn't like to acknowledge enemy victories for good reason, and the Marines most of all didn't like being ordered to stop attacking when Baghdad was but a few days away and the enemy was on the run. We had to allow RCT-1 off to the east to catch up, accomplishing the giant pincer movement. They were in place by April 1, and finally we could move forward.

I told no one that March 30 was my twenty-first birthday. I didn't want the attention; most of all I didn't want to be hazed. I had brought a small bottle of ten-year single-malt Scotch from the States hidden away in my toiletry bag for the occasion, but in a pop inspection in Kuwait, one of our staff NCOs confiscated it and probably drank it. Regardless, I saved a few goodies for the occasion. In the smoke-grenade box on the hull just below my seat I stored away my apricot jelly and a gooey rice-crispy treat that my sister had sent me in Kuwait; it was now almost liquefied. I also saved a can of Pepsi that was piping hot, but I didn't care. I ate the gooey mess, drank the hot Pepsi, and spread the contraband jelly over crackers by myself when no one was looking. It was the best meal I had in weeks. *It's my birthday, dammit!* When most spend the day in a drunken stupor, I spent it fighting for my country. I found it a blessing, though. I would never for the rest of my life forget where I was, or what I was doing on my birthday.

Sitting on the front of the M-88, flies had full access to my smelly uniform. We were still in MOPP 4, which meant wearing a charcoal-lined rubber suit over camouflaged utilities that made you overheat if you stayed inside the M-88 for long. All we had inside was a crappy little fan on a crappy little NBC (nuclear, biological, chemical) system to keep us cool, whereas tankers had a large, effective fan hooked up to their superior NBC system that attached to their suits and helmets, directly cooling their skin. Sometimes I envied them.

Reading old letters, I memorized the words but read them anyway. I didn't receive any new letters from the C-130, but some did. I envied them too. The sand-ridden letters distracted me—anything to focus my mind away from days I didn't wish to remember. I kept one in my left breast pocket the entire war—a motivating letter from my father. I arched my neck at the surround, ignoring the tanks and the large black flies that dominated my reality.

The cloverleaf was a terrible place. It was a wrecked area, like an apartment complex destroyed, earth then piled hastily over it, possibly to cover up a nightmare, but to no avail. Cookware, clothes, pieces of dolls, shoes in the dirt—a terrible feeling resided in that place. People died there. I felt it; and we parked, lived, and burned our waste on that graveyard for days. Unbelievable nightmares wrestled me awake, only to carry into the next one, nearly the same as the last. The swarm of flies attested to something being long dead. I wanted nothing more than to leave that sullen place, even if it meant going into combat once again. I would soon get my wish.

The baser part of me ignored instinct and focused on the few things of beauty that had sprung there. Large thickets of a bristly kind of plant abounded, colored like the desert, camouflaged in its exactness. Flowers of purple and pink grew toward the ground in bushels, like grapes but flowered. Objects of handcrafted beauty were abundant as well. I looked to the ground and picked up a small saucer. Smearing away the dirt, I discovered birds and flowers upon porcelain rimmed with gold. I pictured the teacup on it, ready to be served, now only a cracked remnant.

On the road, a crew of sulking Marines lifted the arms and legs of an Iraqi civilian onto the hood of a Hummer—the same civilian we shot days ago in a car speeding toward our lines. But not before the Marines had a chance to play with him. I recorded the disgusting incident afterward as a letter, wishing I had more rank to stop them:

> I was not angry at Marines since I came to Iraq until this instant. Both of you gave me reason to hate you, hate mankind when I looked over to the dead Iraqi body and saw you toying with it. I had been looking at his lifeless hand dangling from under the tarp for days as I sat there on the M-88. I remember looking at his wedding ring wondering how his family would react...the stupid man should have stopped when we told him. But that didn't stop you. Two Marines, one staff sergeant, and one lance corporal, had propped

up the dead man and threw his arm over their shoulder and were taking pictures. Laughing. Two carnal beings and one deceased posing for the eternal picture. What you did next, my comrades, stuck with me for life. We shot him square in the chest, and you, you disgusting animal, stuck your fingers inside the fibrous hole and roared all the more. I should have stopped you, but you were with a Staff Sergeant, one of our leaders whom we were supposed to trust and admire, and therefore protected from action. I became disgusted with the war in that instant, disgusted with you, and for the rest of my life I will not give you the honor of uttering your name to another living soul. Well done, you idiots.

I watched the wedding band on his lifeless hand as he was driven off to a nameless grave dug by Marines in this nameless desert. I glanced at my saucer once again and my thoughts churned at how fragile our dreams truly could be. I sent up a prayer. I wish I could remember the words.

With time to sit and think, I wondered what was happening on the Iraqi side. On March 31, the Iraqi minister of information, Mohammed Saeed al-Sahaf ("Baghdad Bob"), reported to the Iraqi people and the entire world absolute nonsense.

Those mercenaries of the international gang of villains sent their failing louts, but the snake is trapped in the quagmire now. The lines of communications now extend over 500 kilometers. Our people from all sectors, fighters, courageous tribesmen, as well as fighters from the Arab Socialist Ba'ath Party fought battles and pushed the enemy back into the desert . . . Now hundreds of thousands of the fighters of the valiant Iraq people are distributed in all places. Saddam's Fedayeen and some small units of the Iraqi Armed Forces began to engage the louts of the villains of the US and British colonialism day and night. We have decided not to let them sleep . . . We destroyed 13 tanks, 8 tracked personnel carriers, and 6 half-tracked vehicles.[86]

The Iraqi people and Saddam believed him. When the Iraqis got wind that RCT-5 was waiting at the cloverleaf, the Iraqis claimed victory for holding us at bay, which was ridiculous. We were simply conducting an operational pause to allow the rest of the coalition to catch up. At best, what the Iraqi people and the government heard from their propaganda machine was an amalgamation of lies and half-truths, because no one in the regime would dare report what was actually going on. We were indeed stretched out, but we were intimately organized; we were indeed not sleeping, but that was because of our strategy and not their planning.

Baghdad Bob was a celebrity. There was a pop song about him, an action figure, T-shirts, mugs, and he is quoted beyond measure.[87] He denied that the coalition was gaining any significant hold on Iraq up to the last day. He did his job, and Saddam Hussein could have done no better in appointing him information minister. His audacious, bombastic manner was appreciated by all; even President Bush, who listened to his rhetoric, enjoyed his disinformation.

They're coming to surrender or be burned in their tanks.
We are in control. They are in a state of hysteria.

---

86   FBIS, (31 March 2003) "Iraq's Al-Sahhaf Holds News Conference on Military Situation," Doha Al-Jazirah Satellite Channel Television.
87   Deprang, Emily, *'Baghdad Bob' and His Ridiculous, True Predictions*, March 21, 2013. http://www.theatlantic.com/international/archive/2013/03/baghdad-bob-and-his-ridiculous-true-predictions/274241/

Losers, they think that by killing civilians and trying to distort the feelings of the people they will win. I think they will not win, those bastards.

I would like to clarify a simple fact here: How can you lay siege to a whole country? Who is really under siege now? Baghdad cannot be besieged. Al-Nasiriyah cannot be besieged. Basra cannot be besieged.

They are trapped in Umm Qasr. They are trapped near Basra. They are trapped near Nasiriyah. They are trapped near Najaf. They are trapped everywhere.

They are retarded.

They are not in Najaf. They are nowhere. They are on the moon. They are snakes in the desert.[88]

Those of us in Iraq who had radios heard and laughed at the broadcasts. The purpose of the Iraqi information ministry was to keep the population under control. Aside from the rampant looting I witnessed in Baghdad after its fall, the population had, in fact, been kept from rioting. Baghdad Bob was a tool, and he did a magnificent job keeping Iraqis misinformed even as our tanks sped past them.

I was to learn afterwards that nineteen million leaflets were dropped on Iraq from October 2002 to March 20, 2003; an additional thirty-one million were dropped during the war itself.[89] They contained simple pictures and friendly instructions to stay out of the fighting, that the coalition meant no harm to the Iraqi people. Here are some statements printed on the leaflets:

Who needs you more? Your family or the regime? Return to your home and family.

FOR YOUR SAFETY—Abandon your weapon systems. Whether manned or unmanned, these weapon systems will be destroyed.

---

[88] One of the few websites devoted to Baghdad Bob has a wonderful array of quotes, and even sells T-Shirts, mugs and other items. http://www.welovetheiraqiinformationminister.com/

[89] Hosmer, *Why Iraqi Resistance to the Coalition Invasion was so Weak*, 104.

Do not give your life for Saddam. Do not continue to endure his evil deeds. The coalition is here to help you and your family.[90]

The leaflets had a demoralizing effect on the Iraqi Army. The Americans sometimes dropped them directly on Iraqi military positions, which sowed great fear and alarm. If the Americans could drop leaflets with precision, they easily could have dropped bombs.[91] "The Americans had come halfway across the world to dump their trash on us," one Iraqi officer stated, and it had a terrible effect on morale. Precision bombing after the leaflets showed that the US followed up on its warning and caused mass desertions by all but the most loyal to the regime. It was why we were facing only the most fanatical, loyal fighters; the absence of Iraqi regulars showed the resounding success of psychological operations.

★ ★ ★ ★ ★

The 3rd Infantry Division had been held up battling approximately 2,000 Fedayeen, Ba'ath militia, and foreign fighters in An Najaf from March 25 to 28 in an engagement that was like that of As Samwah earlier.[92] Both engagements centered on securing key bridges across the Euphrates against paramilitary and some regular troops—again, the most loyal remnant of Saddam's forces. Bridges were secured not without detonation and incident, the Fedayeen using human shields and hiding in civilian homes in their resistance. The 101st and 82nd relieved the 3rd Infantry Division on March 29 and 30 to allow them to take Karbala.

In a deep-strike exercise, the 101st Aviation Brigade attacked the Karbala Gap and the 14th Brigade of the Medina Division on March 28 with some success, allowing the 3rd Infantry Division to keep moving. The Army 3rd Infantry Division began its movement

---

90   Friedman, Herbert, *Operation Iraqi Freedom*, accessed October 16, 2015, http://www.psywarrior.com/OpnIraqiFreedom.html
91   Thom Shanker, "Regime Thought War Unlikely, Iraqis Tell U.S.," *The New York Times*, February 12, 2004.
92   Fontenot, *On Point*, 195.

toward the Karbala by March 30. So far, the Army was experiencing what the Marines were—attacks upon armor that were often suicidal and beyond reason. The Army constantly reported running out of ammunition holding back suicidal waves of Fedayeen attacking from civilian vehicles. The Iraqis were often hopped up on drugs or were fighting because they felt they had no choice. It is also possible that they were forced to fight at gunpoint, or their families were being held hostage to induce them to fight. Whatever the case, nearly all of these incidents were carried out by the loyal Fedayeen, Ba'ath militia, or foreign fighters—not the regular army.[93] Precision air attacks effectively silenced the Iraqi Army during the invasion. They deserted en masse across the board. Some, however, still remained.

To the north, on March 26, 954 soldiers of the 173rd Brigade jumped into Bashur Airfield in northern Iraq by way of a C-17. Three days later, approximately 2,000 soldiers were in place, ready for offensive operations. They destroyed multiple Iraqi infantry divisions on their way to Kirkuk, seizing caches of Iraqi gold stores and oil fields essential to the operation. They remained in place in the general area of Kirkuk with their 70,000 allied Peshmerga fighters blocking the retreat of any forces coming from Baghdad. The north was overwhelmed with coalition fighters cutting off the retreat from Baghdad. The north was taken with very few casualties. Only Baghdad and a few cities south of it remained.

---

93   Woods, *Iraqi Perspectives Project*, 130.

Photo of the Author

by Ian D. Fraser Photography

Front view of an M-88 Hercules.

Photo credit: Lance Corporal Desire M. Mora

Rear of M-88 Hercules.

Photo credit: Lance Corporal Austin Mealy

The Hercules removing an engine with its crane. Repairs like this were done all over the field and sometimes under fire where speed was of the essence.

Photo credit: SSGT Grindstaff

Bravo 2nd Tanks guidon.

Photo Credit: LT Sean Gobin of bravo 2nd Tanks

The M-88 A-2 HERCULES Hells Wrecker and the Advanced Vehicular Lift Bridge staged in Kuwait.

Photo credit: SSGT Aaron Grant

Tanks staged in Kuwait the day before invading Iraq.

Photo credit: SSGT Grindstaff of Bravo 2nd Tanks

Terrain Model etched in the sand in Kuwait outlining
the plan to invade Iraq.

Photo credit: SSGT Grindstaff of Bravo 2nd Tanks

Bravo M1-A1 with contraband Old Glory taken down after this photo was taken. Kudos to the crew.

Photo credit: LT Sean Gobin of Bravo 2nd Tanks

Camel crossings literally held up the invasion on multiple occasions.

Photo credit: SSGT Grindstaff of Bravo 2nd Tanks

Curious Iraqi women.

Photo credit: Mr. Andy Cross

The march to Baghdad with RCT-5 from the front seat of Hells Wrecker with the author at his station.

Photo credit: SSGT Aaron Grant

Combat action from the front seat.

Photo credit: SSGT Grindstaff of Bravo 2nd Tanks

First EPW's taken at Rumalia.

Photo credit: Mr. Andy Cross

View of gunners sight in the M1-A1 Abrams Main Battle Tank.

Photo credit: SSGT Grindstaff of Bravo 2nd Tanks

The M1-A1 Abrams Main Battle Tank. The most deadly ground element in Iraq and the tip of the spear on every front.

Photo credit: SSGT Grindstaff of Bravo 2nd Tanks

Oil silos and wells were hit by retreating forces causing huge black towers of smoke all over the Rumalia complex.

Photo credit: CPL William Hayes of Bravo 2nd Tanks

Oil silo on fire in Rumalia.

Photo credit: CPL William Hayes of Bravo 2nd Tanks

Rolling with us was everything from hummers to trucks; AAV's to Tanks packed with the Marines of Bravo, and the fabled Fifth Marines.

Photo credit: SSGT Grindstaff of Bravo 2nd Tanks

Author CPL Aaron Grant in front of a destroyed Iraqi tracked vehicle in the early days of March.

Photo credit: SSGT Aaron Grant

Iraqi Regular's surrendured in mass creating a logistical problem to the Marines in front.

Photo credit: SSGT Grindstaff of Bravo 2nd Tanks

Trench fires were everywhere.

Photo credit: SSGT Grindstaff of Bravo 2nd Tanks

Willie the Pigeon. He landed on smelly Hells Wrecker and lived with us inside for days.

Photo credit: SSGT Aaron Grant

Adobe dwellings that harbored Fedayeen fighters.

Photo credit: Mr. Andy Cross

Combat action on hummer with the Marines of RCT-5 on March 27th.

Photo credit: Mr. Andy Cross

Combat action with the Marines of RCT-5 on March 27th.

Photo Credit: Mr. Andy Cross

Marines of Bravo 2nd Tanks in a firefight in the last days of March.

Photo credit: Mr. Andy Cross

Photo of the Author

by Ian D. Fraser Photography

C-130 touches down on Han'tush Airfield carrying
much needed supplies and especially mail.

An american M1-A1 destroyed in the first days
of April just outside Baghdad.

LT. Brian McPhillips. Universally loved by all especially in Bravo 2nd Tanks. Rest in peace warrior.

Chasing down the enemy off road often mired US armor. The Hells Wrecker recovered many in central Iraq; sometimes under fire. The author is centered.

Photo credit: SSGT Aaron Grant

View of civilians on the march to Baghdad.

Photo credit: SSGT Grindstaff of Bravo 2nd Tanks

Destroyed American humvee hit with an RPG.

Photo credit: SSGT Grindstaff of Bravo 2nd Tanks

Destroyed T-72. It was common for turrets to spin into the air after being hit by the M1-A1 120mm main gun.

Photo credit: LT Stephenson of Bravo 2nd Tanks

Emerging from the desert to brush crowded alleyways in central Iraq caused the Marines to be on extra alert.

Photo credit: CPL William Hayes of Bravo 2nd Tanks

Destroyed Iraqi tracked vehicle outside Baghdad.

Photo credit: SSGT Grindstaff of Bravo 2nd Tanks

Marines got sleep whenever and wherever they could, here is Bravo mechanic CPL Watson fast asleep in the turret of an Abrams.

Photo credit: SSGT Hoffa of Bravo 2nd Tanks

M1-A1 Abrams with mine plow.

Photo credit: CPL William Hayes of Bravo 2nd Tanks

Stuck Hells Wrecker and a Bravo tank at Sayib Abd that caused the crews to be displaced for the duration of the war.

Photo credit: CPL William Hayes of Bravo 2nd Tanks

The final resting place of Hells Wrecker at Sayib Abd.
Photo credit: TECOM USMC

EPW's taken just outside Baghadad.
Photo credit: SSGT Grindstaff of Bravo 2nd Tanks

The impoverished Saddam City just outside Baghdad. The sight of it strengthened the resolve of all the Marines who saw it.

Photo credit: CPL William Hayes of Bravo 2nd Tanks

The Iraqis loved to watch us pass by; crowding the Marines when they stopped for a high-five and souvenirs.

Photo credit: SSGT Grindstaff of Bravo 2nd Tanks

Baghdad streets with cheering civilians.
Ever-present danger didn't seem to bother them.

Photo credit: CPL William Hayes of Bravo 2nd Tanks

An example of the aged tanks that Saddam utilized.
Here is a WW2 Sherman Tank in Baghdad.

Photo credit: LT Stephenson of Bravo 2nd Tanks

Looting Iraqis in Baghdad. There was little one could do to stop them as the local police had disrobed for fear of being shot.

Photo credit: CPL William Hayes of Bravo 2nd Tanks

Typical adulation of Saddam Hussein painted in Baghdad which passing Marines loved to pepper with holes.

Photo credit: SGT Erikson of 2nd Tanks

SCUD Launcher placed next to Baghdad University. Saddam loved to hide his equipment near schools and hospitals because the Americans avoided targeting them.

Photo credit: SSGT Aaron Grant

Civilians peddling wares while setting up base in Baghdad.

Photo credit: CPL William Hayes of Bravo 2nd Tanks

Happy Iraqi children encountered in Baghdad.

Photo credit: SSGT Grindstaff of Bravo 2nd Tanks

Iraqi children in Baghdad.

Photo credit: CPL William Hayes of Bravo 2nd Tanks

Memorial service held in Camp Lejeune for Marines killed Iraq in the 2003 Invasion.

Photo credit:
SSGT Aaron Grant

CHAPTER VII

HELLS WRECKER DIES

*Everything in war is simple,
but even the simplest thing is difficult.*
CARL VON CLAUSEWITZ

THE LAND HAD CHANGED. From the desert we emerged to a land of green palm trees and fertile soil. The dirt roads we patrolled were flanked by high brush that made us nervous. There were places on the Tigris that could easily conceal the enemy. Some roads near An Nu'maniyah were as wide as a tank, and the bristly undergrowth scraped either side, twigs snapping off into our hatches. I was on high alert for good reason.

It was April 2, and we had passed through An Nu'maniyah with ease thanks to 1st Battalion, 5th Marines. The day before, they attacked along Route 27 and destroyed a company-sized unit over the Saddam Canal fully equipped with defensive positions and bunkers. The bridge had not been detonated, which made no sense to me because we were so close to Baghdad; surely our enemy was aware of our intentions. Bravo Company led the charge through the lines after the bridge was taken and crossed over the Tigris afterward, where we suffered a loss. Receiving sporadic sniper fire along the route, one of our tanks was hit on the exterior fuel bladder, spilling over the engine compartment, causing a catastrophic fire. The crew narrowly escaped a fiery death. I passed the inferno in Hells Wrecker not knowing what happened or if anyone was dying. The rounds were cooking off by the time we left, receiving an order to rescue mired tanks not far from Al 'Aziziyah at Sayyib Abd.

Hells Wrecker was designed to pull mired vehicles out of hazards. Most of the time, tanks in Iraq got themselves stuck in the mud when their overzealous commanders pursued the enemy through farmers' fields or where there were shoddy roads unable to hold a seventy-ton tank. It's easy to mire a tank because it's so heavy, especially in muddy fields. With its main winch capable of pulling 140 tons of dead weight, our M-88 could free tanks and anything else stuck in the mud. If we were rescuing a Hummer, we hoisted the crane, or "boom," as we call it, directly over the vehicle, lowered the cable, and lifted until the vehicle dangled in midair. A tank was nearly as easy, except we had to be mindful of the type of surface we were on. We rarely came across anything we could not move—except when we had a malfunction. And that was exactly what happened.

Rolling up, we came upon a sorry sight indeed. Two of our tanks were mired in three feet of mud in the middle of a field. One had gone in, gotten stuck, and another trying to retrieve it had gotten stuck as well. We were directed to rescue them even as the rest of our company was moving north. We had to think fast. We were not under fire, but that could change at the drop of a hat. Our commander decided to go in right after them in the same manner as they had. I protested, saying we would just get stuck as they did, but he didn't listen. He was under pressure to recover the M1-A1s as soon as possible, so he decided to risk it. The enemy was still out there, and every bit of ruckus we made brought him closer to us. We had to move fast.

The roar and twist of the M-88 track spit chunks of mud thirty feet into the air. Entering the field, Hells Wrecker fought itself, jerking madly at the slick earth, which sucked it further down in every attempt the driver made to free it. Mud encroached to the very doors, normally five feet above the ground, and the noble effort to save the stuck M1-A1s threatened to bury Hells Wrecker entirely. I felt as if my seat was sinking as the M-88 moved inches forward and finally came to a complete stop, tracks sliding in the earth, doing nothing except burning fuel.

The dozen Marines on the scene knew what needed to be done. We deployed our collapsible shovels called E-Tools and started hacking at the earth around the M-88. The sergeants directed as we used the small shovels to heave, and we dug until nightfall until our arms gave out. We were sweaty and covered with mud, and I was miserably tired. We succeeded in moving much of the earth, but the M-88 was bottomed-out on clay, and no matter what we did, it kept sinking. Help would have to wait until morning.

That night while readying my bed I looked up at the stars and saw the constellation Orion. The brilliant heavens comforted me even though I was half a world away from everything I knew. God was watching. Like a lightning rod, I whispered a prayer, grounding myself to what was important. I wish I could remember the words. Even then, in the most uncertain of times, when the rest of our company was fighting north, He knew our needs, and as I awoke the next morning, I realized the full measure of divine protection. Three stuck tanks in the heart of Iraq lay in the field with a dozen or so Marines exhausted from the march. We had slept through the night. A guard was placed when I went to sleep, and when I awoke the next morning *everyone* was sleeping. In a fit of rage, I woke everyone up. Sleeping while on duty used to be a hanging offense because it endangered not just your life but everyone else's you had sworn to protect. God spared us that night. The Iraqis seemed to have no idea we were there. I did not see it at the time, but now I know this instance was yet another example where God preserved me and the Marines from danger. "There by the Grace of God go I," a wise man once said, and by Grace we continued north the next day.

Battlefield Prayers

Not a single one of them I remember.
   The bullets and grenades blot out memory where God should be.
No, the days were long, and
   The moment I sent them up they were forgotten to me, but
     Remembered by God.
Once I nearly felt my heart leap out of my chest at God,
   Uttering the most meaningful prayer of my life.
But for now,
   Though I remember emotion; fiercely connected to Providence,
   I have to content myself with the knowledge He will reveal when I meet:
The day all my battlefield prayers will be revealed.

Our rescuers arrived; infantry from the bellies of two amtracks had only a few precious hours to help before rejoining the fight north. Heaving and taking turns, the Marines met the challenge. Shovels struck the earth near the elevated portions of the track, and my own hands became brown extensions, like theirs, resembling the rest of the scene, colors fading into the mud. The plan was simple—recover the less-wedged Hells Wrecker, which had the awesome torque to recover the other M1-A1s in worse condition.

Things were not going well, and time was running out. Hells Wrecker lurched from side to side as I hung upside down below the commander's seat trying to see what was wrong with the main winch. I had no idea what I was doing. I had never worked on an M-88 main winch before, but I was turning a wrench nonetheless. Hydraulic fluid soon covered me, and miserably I emerged without success. The M-88 wasn't going anywhere. Orders were soon received to strip Hells Wrecker and the other tanks of sensitive material and join the company north.

It was at that moment my face went cold. Flush, no doubt, as if I had seen a ghost. In front of me were three tanks hopelessly stuck in the middle of Iraq, and all of the sudden I realized my error. *Could it be? Is this my fault?* I rushed up to my seat on the M-88, and when no one was looking, I pulled out of the smoke-grenade box containing my nasty little secret. The apricot jelly. Half eaten, it was liquefied and hot in my hand. Thrusting it immediately into my pocket, my eyes bulged. If anyone knew of this, I would be hazed until I passed out or worse; it would all be blamed on me, and I would never live it down. Inching away from the Marines, I neared the tree line, not so far as to be noticed but far enough so no one could see what I was doing. In seconds, I pulled the jelly from my pocket and pitched it out into the woods. Done. I was now a believer. I was now a superstitious lout like the rest of them. Owing to this experience, I would never eat or touch an apricot again.

Hells Wrecker was my home, and I was now homeless. I stripped the maps from my rigger's seat, took down the photos of my family and felt my heart sink. We stripped our weapons, our dirty M2, and all the AT-4s and loaded them up on the amtrack. We ripped out the radio, our tools, and our Alice-packs and loaded them up as well. The homeless tankers and mechanics sulked in the foreign hull, fatigued and demoralized. The watertight gate closed, and I sat next to Marines I had never met, in the belly of a beast I had no control over. I didn't even have communications. No more would I view the war from the front seat of my beloved M-88; no more would I hear the war except by the rumbling of the amtrack and the occasional view I had from my seat when I could stand. I would now view the war like most of the Marines—crammed together elbow to elbow with little to no knowledge of what was going on outside. All I knew was that I had to be prepared in the event the gate slammed down for combat. Outside having my gear and weapons ready, there was nothing to do in the belly of the beast except sleep. Marines had to shout over the noise of the engine just to be heard, so most just stood on their seats, peeping out the top for something to do; the lucky ones found something to shoot at. This was my new home and I had to get used to it.

The metal seat was merciless. My bottom half had no feeling after the eight-hour trip skirting the Tigris River, and to top it off everything reeked of diesel and exhaust within. When a Marine got tired of standing on his seat looking out the top, I excitedly took my turn to allow blood to flow to my legs. Rifle pointed out, I stood for hours until I beheld a sight indeed. Ponds of blood-red water lay outside a massive mud-brick town on the outskirts of Baghdad. Saddam City. This was where the oppressed Shia Arabs lived, and I was appalled by the poverty of the people I saw living in little more than mud holes in the ground. If they had electricity, a single pole was jerry-rigged with hundreds of little wires draping down to various homes. Seeing the oppressed watching the Americans pass by strengthened my resolve. We represented a new beginning, throwing humanitarian rations and water bottles in the midst of shouts of joy.

Americans had no concept of such poverty, and I sent up a prayer thanking God for the bounty I had, that I did not have to drink from a blood-red pool, and that I would never have to live with such oppression. Eighteenth-century Enlightenment scholar Mary Montagu said, "There is a remarkable difference between the cities of a republic and those of an absolutist." And here was the greatest poverty I had seen. Shia ghettos like these were favorite tramping grounds for Saddam's secret police. It made my heart ache knowing there were children, babies in there who had no idea why they were so abused, or why their friends and relatives disappeared from their lives forever. Saddam needed to go.

The gate opened ten miles from Baghdad, just north of the Tigris. I stretched out in the sand using my Alice-pack as a pillow. Much had happened since I left Hells Wrecker at Sayyib Abd. The last few days saw the tightening of the noose on Baghdad. The Army 3rd Infantry Division moved to breach the Karbala, while the 101st Airborne made a feint to Hillah while seizing and securing Najaf. Iraqi units at Karbala Gap shot down an Army H-60 Black Hawk helicopter, killing seven and wounding four others.[94] To the east, the Iron Horse was the first unit to cross the Tigris River at An Nu'maniyah and came into enemy contact the same day. A battalion-sized reinforced Iraqi unit waited in the vicinity of the bridge crossing on Route 27, and the tanks made quick work of them, destroying one T-55, eight BMPs, eleven military vehicles, five antiaircraft guns, and approximately 120 troops.[95] Apparently, some of the vehicles had been abandoned thanks to precision bombing, but there was resistance nonetheless where the enemy felt confident enough to attack the tanks from a distance. Only one friendly tank was immobilized. The tanks kept moving through the night to throw the Al Nida Armored Division off balance.

Civilians crowded at the roadblock to our lines, and I went out to investigate. "Mister! Mister!" they shouted, holding up cigarettes and bottles full of liquor. I approached, watching many Marines buying up their wares, and the Iraqis, giddy with excitement, ran off as fast as they could to get more. Among the flow of valuable supplies like cigarettes and fresh food to our lines, we were surprised and unprepared for the influx of Iraqi paper money that the civilians sold to troops eager for a souvenir. Of course, the price for these bills was outrageous, but it was the image of Saddam they were peddling—a dead currency useless to them but interesting to us. I bought a few myself. They were able to live off of fifty dollars in a month when Americans couldn't seem to get by on thousands; American troops hence became a golden opportunity of supply and demand to the Iraqi. The drive for profit brought the Iraqi civilian from the safety of his home into the theater of war. Indeed, the war itself had temporarily destroyed the commercial system of Iraq and it was all people could do to fill their diesel engines and make it to the market. The Saddam Iraq dinar was worthless, and the US dollar, for the time being, became the popular currency of the Iraqi people, straight from

---

94 The Encyclopedia of Middle East Wars: The United States in the Persian Gulf, Afghanistan, and Iraq Conflicts, Spencer C. Tucker, p. 672, ABC-CLIO, 2010
95 2nd Tank Battalion After Action Report, 8.

American soldiers' pockets. US troops instantly became celebrated not only for liberating them from Saddam but also because they had viable currency.

It became common knowledge among Marines that many Iraqis were out of work. Data from the CIA in 2003 states that the unemployment rate was nearly 28 percent at the time,[96] an approximation that was evident on the ground as sentries posted to protect the bases were inundated with desperate people. The economy depended upon Iraq's ability to produce oil and other less global-affecting products like cement, and the war was like a cardiac arrest to this production.

No Marine I knew carried less than fifty US dollars, and there were thousands of us on the front. The Iraqis brought the worst liquor, the most disgusting cigarettes (the blue-packaged *Sumer* was a popular brand) and the most terrible prices to the table in exchange for a chance to make off with a profit. By the time a case of cigarettes was bought by a nicotine-starved Marine, it had gone through many hands. From the lowly merchant to the running Iraqi boy, who then handed it off in relay to another, and another, to the front line wherever it happened to be. Since no one could read Arabic, it was impossible to know what the original price of anything was, but judging by the thin, tasteless tobacco and the retch of rum in one's throat, it could not have been much.

"I wouldn't pay five bucks for this bottle in the States!" and "These cigs are crap" were popular mantras among the Marines. Yet we kept buying. Our money was useless to us because our bellies were full of rations. There was no market, convenience store, or souvenir shop in an invasion. It was so useless to us that I recall being tempted to burn a twenty to get some kindling going in the middle of a cold desert night. A story circulated of an addicted Marine so desperate for a

---

96   Central Intelligence Agency, *Iraq Economic Data* (1989-2003), Regime Finance and Procurement – Annex D, https://www.cia.gov/library/reports/general-reports-1/iraq_wmd_2004/chap2_annxD.html

draw he rolled up *tea grounds* in a bill and then smoked it. Most of us were therefore glad to pay for the dry, nasty Sumer.

Since landing in Kuwait, a micro-economy of government-supplied rations erupted as the medium of exchange on the front between Marines, and now it was the same for the Iraqis, who traded souvenirs for them. The MRE package (meal ready to eat) came to us in familiar cases of twelve with up to twenty-four different variations of meals depending upon which case one received. Meals like cheese tortellini, meatloaf with gravy, and chicken with rice were bartered between Marines, and the prices fluctuated with demand. Meals contained valuable contents like pound cake and powdered milkshake, Skittles, M&M's, and even toilet paper, which had obvious use on the front. My own pocket was full of the toilet paper packs. Hoards of stashed goods from a rucksack or greasy tank appeared when supplies of "the good stuff" waned and the would-be businessmen among us could make off with a profit in dollars or cigarettes. Marines would give an entire meal for the legendary strawberry shake and even more for a lemon-flavored pound cake.

Yellow-packaged humanitarian rations were passed to the Iraqis, and they, thinking that they were being traded for something, didn't understand that we were *giving* them something to eat. They opened them immediately and found attractive labels such as rice pilaf, crackers, and candy. The Marines had sampled the freebies and discovered what we were handing out was better than our MREs. By the war's end our stash of yellow-packaged rations was gone, not because we gave them all out to Iraqis but because we stuffed our faces with the superior food within. We all agreed that it was ridiculous that our own government would give better food to the Iraqis than to us. The consequence? The Iraqis got the nastiest meals we didn't want out of our own supplies—like the infamous pork-chop MRE, thrown to them fully knowing it was against their religion as we ate like kings.

★ ★ ★ ★ ★

The 2nd Tank Battalion attacked along Route 6 toward Al Aziziyah and encountered ambush tactics in the vicinity of Al Battikh. During the battle that followed, the Iron Horse wiped out the Al Nida Division, destroying a whopping dozen tanks, thirty-three BMPs, thirty-one artillery pieces, thirty-nine AAA systems, twenty-five military trucks, nine bunker complexes, and a myriad of other military targets with the help of Apache and AH-1W Super Cobra attack helicopters. Scattered across the countryside were the smoldering remains of tanks and troops who dared to occupy them. While the Iron Horse was busy at Al Battikh, 3rd Battalion, 5th Marines was engaged in bitter street fighting against the remnants of Al Nida in Al Aziziyah. From defensive positions along the highway and within the city, the conventional forces there were the most motivated, organized and supplied yet. Supported by foreign fighters, the Republican Guard stopped the advance of India Company for eight hours of close combat while wounding two Marines and killing another.[97]

All along Route 6 and within Al Aziziyah the radio screamed that tanks needed help. The cursed fields in the area trapped the tracks in mud until the tanks "bottomed out," creating a hazard for recovery crews who had to work around enemy fire. Hercules crews responded, connecting the down tank with the 120-ton snatch block and threading the three-inch round main winch cable through it to double up on pulling strength. The driver of the Hercules then activated the winch from stable ground, dragging the victim through the mud until the tank's track was able to make it the rest of the way; it was all in a day's work, and all in a combat zone.

The AH-1W Cobras overhead harassed the enemy, making things a little easier for those on the ground. Another tank's transmission froze, and with no safe zone to repair it, another friendly M1-A1 backed up to it and connected tow bars and hurriedly towed it out of the hot zone. The Republican Guard scored a hit on another's

---

[97] Regimental Combat Team 5 Narrative Summary, United States Marine Corps, actions of April 3–4.

track, effectively taking it out of service as the tank could no longer move. It would be at least a day before Al Aziziyah was clear and the defenders gave up—one of the worst days for American armor in the entire war.[98]

The last organized attempt to defeat the American forces came in the early morning of April 3. Iraqi lieutenant general Hamdani, who had fought in five previous wars, collected a group of fifteen T-72 tanks, forty armored personnel carriers, infantry, and artillery to make a final effort to retake a section of Baghdad. US tanks picked them off at 3,000 meters in the middle of the night, like a video game. A single tank company accomplished this task without a single loss of life due to the Iraqis' lack of night vision optics coupled with aged equipment. The general nearly fought to the last man for "the honor of Iraq and the fate of Baghdad."[99]

Only a day's march from Baghdad, the Iraqis finally had the gumption to try to stop us. They concentrated along Highway 6 to Baghdad. From fighting positions in lines of trenches, from buildings along the road, from dense green vegetation, they shot at the convoy with small arms, popping up in black-clad and olive-green uniforms just long enough to make resistance. Hundreds of them hunkered in well-prepared defensive positions, which slowed the convoy and the foray into Al Aziziyah. The close air support was impeccable; the Marines' best friend was the exceptionally tough Fairchild Republic A-10 Thunderbolt II "Warthog," a fixed-wing jet from the end of the Vietnam era; it used its 30 mm rotary cannon, sweeping the defensive positions. The ground danced around the fighters at 4,000 rounds a minute. The low-level *brrrrrt* of the cannon above the Marines' heads was unmistakable, and a godsend in battle. Later, combing through the bodies and the POWs, Marines learned that several hundred fighters from Syria, Sudan, Jordan, Lebanon, Egypt,

---

98   Colonel Reynolds, Nicholas USMCR, *U.S. Marines in Iraq, 2003 Basrah, Baghdad And Beyond: U.S. Marines in the Global War on Terrorism*, 94.
99   Lieutenant-General Hamdani interview via Stephen Hosmer, 2004.

and even Iran augmented the Republican Guard.[100]

To the north, Army Special Forces and Kurdish Peshmerga fighters had the glory of holding off a battalion-sized unit of Republican Guards at the Battle of Debecka Pass on April 6. Two-hundred fifty Iraqis with armor and tanks faced a mere thirty Americans and eighty motivated Kurds who had nothing larger than a five-ton truck; the odds were nearly three to one.[101] The Iraqis had dug in fighting positions that were a decade old on a ridge overlooking Kurdish territory in Debecka, between Mosul and Kirkuk at a crucial crossroads that needed to be secured to impede Iraqi movement north and provide American access to crucial oil fields. A-teams Alpha 391 and 392 defended a plateau above Highway 2, refusing to give up any ground to the Iraqis. "We all made a mental promise; nobody had to yell out commands. Everybody just knew. We were not going to move back from that point. We were not going to give up that ground. We called that spot 'the Alamo,'" Staff Sergeant Jeffrey Adamec said, later receiving a Silver Star for gallantry.[102] The soldiers killed at least fifty Iraqis using M2 machine guns, small arms, and Javelin missiles, denying the enemy any ground. Adamec later said,

> I don't know who the commander of the enemy unit was, but he'd send out four tanks and four Armored Personnel Carriers, and then when he didn't hear from them, he'd send more. They kept sending guys for the next eight or nine hours. It was odd, like shooting fish in a bucket. This was the worst tactic I'd ever seen. They had no idea we had the Javelins and that we had air support. They were just walking into a bad situation. We could see all the way across

---

100   Regimental Combat Team 5 Narrative Summary, United States Marine Corps, actions of April 3–4. 2nd Tank Battalion Command Chronology, 10.
101   Larson, Chuck Ed., Heroes Among Us, NAL Caliber, 2008, 217.
102   Dyhouse, Tim, *'Black Ops' Shine in Iraq War*, The VFW Magazine: War in Iraq Tribute to the Troops 2003-2011, 2013, p. 27.

the open valley the enemy had to cross. The enemy was not trying to skirt around the Debecka Valley. They came straight across, right at us, head-on, every time.[103]

Major Curtis Hubbard, CO of the 3rd Special Forces Group, C, said, "Two guys shut down the attack. Two guys turned an organized Iraqi attack into chaos. They halted an entire motorized rifle company."[104] It was indeed two men that did the majority of fighting—Adamec and Staff Sergeant Jason Brown. Air support pounded Iraqi positions while the two engaged, and all was well until a bomb was dropped on friendly Kurdish militia, killing seventeen—a catastrophic accident that was not equaled at any other time in the war.[105] "I can't even explain it," Adamec said. "Guys were blown to pieces. Ammo was exploding all around us. Everything was on fire. My pants were soaked with blood."[106] Nonetheless, American and Kurdish determination scattered the enemy in Debecka—a heroic victory that resonated through the ranks—and the pass was secured.

---

103   Larson, Chuck Ed., *Heroes Among Us*, NAL Caliber, 2008, 215.
104   Larson, Chuck Ed., *Heroes Among Us*, NAL Caliber, 2008, 209-210.
105   Dyhouse, Black Ops, 27
106   Larson, *Heroes*, 217.

CHAPTER VIII

Taking Baghdad

THE FIRST TASK OF the 3rd Infantry Division was to seize the Saddam International Airport. They had passed clear through Karbala, taking a series of key roads and bridges, and were attacking the airport to secure it as a staging point for incursions into Baghdad. Surrounded by a fifteen-foot masonry wall and a complement of tanks and dismounts, the airfield posed a significant challenge as the attack commenced under a sliver of moonlight. But breeching the wall in one place and crushing a gate made the airfield easy pickings at midnight. It wasn't until 0200 that the Iraqis noticed the large complement of American armor on their turf, which they attacked with mortars, RPGs and small arms, firing sporadically throughout the rest of the night until daybreak. When the Bandits of B/3-7, C/2-7 Rock, and Task Force 3-69 accompanying them realized they were among the enemy, the soldiers quickly rushed the scattered enemy bunkers, tossing in grenades as they were too well built and too close to destroy with main gun rounds. The bewildered enemy gave up in droves. It would take another two days to secure the airfield as more and more bunkers and secret passageways were discovered, coupled with the immediate threat of the Special Republican Guard (SRG) right outside the perimeter.[107]

"The enemy was all around," according to the TF 2-7 unit history. A FOX chemical reconnaissance vehicle was nearly hit with a main gun round from a hidden T-72, and a Bradley sent to investigate suffered a direct hit, sending shrapnel and gear flying all over the road. The commander was thrown out of the vehicle and his quick-acting driver backed out of sight, saving the rest of the crew from another main gun round. Four soldiers armed with Javelins crept up on no less than three T-72s and, firing, sent turrets flying fifty feet into the air with ammunition cooking off in a fiery inferno.[108] The Iraqis sent more mortars down in the middle of the airfield, trying to hit anything they could. A Bradley with a 25 mm chain gun destroyed the bunker as more Iraqi tanks arrived only to be pounded by an Abrams.

Desert Storm veteran Sergeant First Class Paul Smith and his imbedded company of B/11th Engineers were hurriedly setting up a containment area for EPWs close by when suddenly a hundred Iraqi SRG stormed a nearby tower, firing RPGs and small arms into the soldiers, instantly wounding three and creating chaos. As the Iraqis rushed a nearby gate, Smith took cover next to a wall and lobbed a grenade, halting the enemy for enough time to drag the wounded to cover. He then jumped on a nearby armored personnel carrier and backed into the center of the compound and, fully exposed, jumped into the commander's seat, using the mounted M2 .50 caliber machine gun on the tower and those rushing the gate to great effect. Enemy fire was ferocious, and First Sergeant Smith was mortally wounded defending the task force from an attack that would have been successful had he not selflessly given his life. Bill Smith, his father, recollected a conversation with one of the soldiers on the ground that day.

---

107   Colonel Fontenot, Gregory, Lt Colonel E.J. Degen, and Lt Colonel David Tohn, *On Point: The United States Army in Operation Iraqi Freedom*, 304.
108   TF 2-7 IN Unit History, April 4, 2003.

I spoke with Sergeant Timothy Campbell quite a bit and he told me that when they removed Paul from the armored personnel carrier, he had thirteen holes in his armor vest where the rounds had hit him. He was aware that he was being hit but he chose to stay on that gun. He could have dropped inside the APC and been protected.[109]

Posthumously given the Medal of Honor, his heroic death and uncommon valor resulted in countless lives saved and as many as fifty enemy dead, allowing the airfield to be secured and the mission to Baghdad to continue.[110]

While the fight at the airport erupted on the radio waves, the Army's Apache 3-7 Cavalry moved north and west on April 3, skirting the capital and capturing the intersection of Highways 1 and 10 with relative ease until the enemy got wind the Americans were due west. The Hammurabi Division split up on its way to the airport, sending tanks, trucks, buses, and pickup trucks full of men to the intersection. The Bradleys and M1s in position with the help of close air support and artillery completely destroyed the Iraqi detachment, leaving six T-72s and an armored fighting vehicle smoldering. Not far off and close to the city, air support spotted a whopping twenty T-72s in well-prepared fighting positions. The Army responded, calling on A-10 Warthogs, artillery, and British Tornadoes, and peppering the ground on which the Iraqi battalion lay. Through the fierce barrage and smoke, the cavalry spotted the enemy tanks and engaged them all from the highway; in fifteen minutes, the entire battalion of Republican Guard tanks were ablaze, the Americans not losing a single life or vehicle to Iraqi artillery, mortar, or tank fire.[111]

---

109   Larson, *Heroes*, 193.
110   MOH Citation for Sergeant First Class Paul Smith, Home Of Heroes, http://www.homeofheroes.com/moh/citations_WOT/smith_paul.html, accessed March 19, 2017.
111   Colonel Fontenot, Gregory, Lt Colonel E.J. Degen, and Lt Colonel David Tohn, *On Point: The United States Army in Operation Iraqi Freedom*, 310-311.

While the airport was finally brought under control to the south, Task Force 2-69 advanced through the intersection at 1 and 10 on April 6 and immediately encountered small arms fire. The last objective was to seize several intersections northwest of Baghdad, effectively cutting off all routes of escape. After destroying several tanks, rocket launchers and BMPs, 2-69 beheld an astonishing sight. Directly on the road Iraqis were frantically stripping off their uniforms in full view of the convoy. As they made no motion to surrender, the lead tank mowed them down and sped past to secure the rest of the northwest intersections with little resistance. At the end of the day, the Army had secured everything south and west of the city. None could have anticipated that three days later Baghdad would fall.

★ ★ ★ ★ ★

To the east, the Marines lost an outstanding leader to Iraqi sniper fire. Attacking along Highway 6 on April 4, 2nd Tank Battalion's scout platoon was ambushed, and in the fight that followed, First Lieutenant Brian McPhillips from Pembroke, Massachusetts, standing in the gunner's position, was shot and instantly killed.[112] The scouts then pulled back as Charlie Company tanks filled the void, killing everything in their path. The lieutenant had just taken over command of the platoon and was previously a Bravo Company tank commander whom I considered a kindred spirit. He was the first in 2nd Tanks to be killed in the war; until that time, we all thought ourselves invincible.

"He shouldn't have even been up there," one of his former tankers said to me. "He should have been in the tanks with us and this would never have happened." His death dealt a severe blow to morale as he was universally loved. The tankers wanted to be with him, recalling the days spent with him on Camp Lejeune, as he wasn't overbearing and was frequently seen doing the same menial tasks as his men. He never told anybody to do anything he wasn't willing to do himself,

---
112   2nd Tank Battalion Command Chronology, 10.

and by all standards he was an exemplary Marine. *How could he have died at the hands of these piss-poor shooting Iraqis?* I asked myself.

I felt most for his true friends—the tankers and his family back home. If he was a fraction of what I knew him to be, then how much greater was his loss to those he commanded, befriended, and those he loved?

Tankers and tank mechanics were universally struck that day, and I remember a quiet hush whenever his name was spoken, as if it were contraband, taboo, or we could pretend the horrible event never happened. Sadness was replaced by frustration, then anger—at least in me; I wanted to pour rounds into the enemy as I did days earlier. "Press on," he would say, and indeed we did, with more fervor than we previously mustered.

He wasn't the last to be killed, either. That same day and near the same position, a lead tank was hit with multiple RPGs and one deflected down into the loader's hatch, instantly killing Corporal Bernard Gooden. The fight to cordon Baghdad was getting fiercer and casualties were mounting. Marines considered Bernard's death to be a one-in-a-million shot. He was also loved by those he served with. Marines that knew him recalled how intelligent he was, calling him "Jamaica" because of his accent. I did not have the pleasure of knowing him, though I recall his chiseled Marine features in passing, a look of seriousness and devotion to duty. By the end of that day, 2nd Tank Battalion felt their own mortality and exposure in the loss of these two outstanding Marines. Each man who knew them had their own story, and it was common to hear the recollections in pauses between the fighting or late at night when prayers were sent up. Sending up my own, it was humbling to know I could have easily traded places with these men; we were all in danger. April 4 was not finished with the Iron Horse.

Not far from these fatalities, Charlie Company's tanks were under fierce small arms fire on Highway 6 where the company commander's tank was stalled and immobilized. Captain Jeffery

Houston, descendant of Sam Houston, hopped out of his tank in the middle of a firefight to commandeer another and was immediately shot in the jaw. His driver, Lance Corporal Billy Peixotto, joined him on the ground and with extreme bravery applied pressure to the captain's bleeding face while simultaneously firing at the enemy concealed in ditches all around. Within seconds Charlie Company surrounded the captain with vehicles and medical aid. Cobras fired overhead of the injured captain, keeping the motivated Iraqis who were trying to capitalize on the situation at bay. Marines from amtracks spilled out on either side of the road, killing militia and regulars who appeared to be hopped up on drugs, having to be shot many times before hitting the ground. The mounting American casualties were stalled, and the tanks and infantry cleared the threat before being told to continue north.

For eight hours straight on April 4, 3rd Battalion, 5th Marines following the tanks engaged the enemy in close combat, all the way to the Diyala River east of Baghdad near the Al Nida Republican Guard Command Center. The river was the last main obstacle on the way to Baghdad, running roughly from the north to the southeast and meeting up with the Tigris. Still, 120 mm mortars were dropped on the Marines as the nearby Al Nida Barracks came into view. Sporadic RPG and small arms fire was absorbed by the convoy as it approached a token resistance outside Baghdad. Scattering the enemy, the convoy consolidated without injury, but not before the greatest prize of the day drove right into them.

Coming at a high speed directly for the tanks was an Iraqi civilian vehicle; with seconds to react, multiple vehicles in the convoy opened fire, decimating the passengers. The car screeched to a halt. Two dead men fell out. The Marines discovered that one was a Republican Guard general, probably the one in charge of the base they had just taken. Multiple fighting positions around the base containing motivated Iraqi soldiers were serviced with the help of Cobras overhead, and the whole scene of death and fire calmed down as the day drew to a close.[113]

There was a problem at the Diyala River, the Marines quickly realized the next day. Reconnaissance of suitable bridge crossing sites proved none were viable. When 1st LAR (light armored reconnaissance) approached the bridges, they were met with small arms and mortar fire each time. None were sturdy enough to hold the tanks, even if they passed over them one at a time, which had been done earlier in the south when enemy contact was likely. The solution was simple; the convoy had an AVLB (advanced vehicular lift bridge) with a massive hydraulic boom scissoring out a huge bridge over a sixty-foot gap, allowing heavy tanks to cross over. Outside this advantage, the convoy was also equipped with amphibious vehicles (AAVs), making the crossing relatively easy in the days to come.

The timing was perfect. The Marines in the east and the Army in the west were consolidating, making final checks on ammunition and equipment. It was time for the prize, and Americans everywhere chomped at the bit. Baghdad was surrounded. I was northeast of the city, cleaning my rifle for the fight to come, not realizing that April 8 would be the day the Marines would link up with the Army in Baghdad. It was the first time I heard the phrase "Thunder Run." Marines all around mounted up in tracks and tanks, and I watched them depart with sheer motivation, all the while wishing I still had Hells Wrecker to join in.

One Iraqi general stated that when the tanks arrived in Baghdad "none of us could believe it; it was impossible, we thought."[114] The Army 3rd Infantry Division's tanks made forays into the city, where, after covering nearly 1000 km, they drove through the city's main highways, destroying bunkers and unsuspecting armored vehicles in their path. Iraqi forces were startled from their breakfast and card games. Iraqi news media had broadcasted that the southern campaign was going well against the Americans; pro-Iraqi propaganda now proved utterly false.

---

113   5th Marines Command Chronology, 10.
114   Hosmer, *Iraqi Resistance*, 110.

Iraqi armor was mostly abandoned or destroyed by US air strikes by the time the tanks arrived, but it did not stop some loyal fighters from resisting. These were in most cases jihadist militia and Saddam's special guard, the Fedayeen Saddam. One of the fighters later recounted,

> The fighting was fierce. They had planes and tanks, and all we had were machine-guns, rocket-propelled grenades, and hand grenades... we had to withdraw. We just couldn't stand up to them. There were only about twenty-five of us left. Most of the Fedayeen were killed.[115]

The Marines in the east crossed the Diyala under heavy fire until the Iraqis saw the AAVs drive straight into the river. It caused an instant drop in Iraqi morale; as another fighter later recounted, "When we saw the tanks floating across the river, we knew we could not win against the Americans."[116] Resistance faded into the city.

The Army to the west had already made multiple thunder runs into the city. As our intelligence had trouble assessing the threat within from the beginning, the tanks made quick, knife-like thrusts into the very heart of Baghdad. News media following as close as they could, broadcasting in real time, minutes passed and familiar shots rang out against heavily armored hulls; small arms, which the Iraqis appeared to have no shortage of, once again played a primary role. Civilian vehicles choked the highways, adding an unstable element to an already hazardous situation. Such was the mass of people that they were inevitably caught in the action. Upon destroying an enemy technical vehicle, one officer recalled how an innocent family suffered from the blast, injuring a father and several children. It was

---

115   Ibid., "The Invasion of Iraq: An Oral History," Frontline Transcript, PBS, March 9, 2004.
116   1st Marine Division Command Chronology, Jan-Jun03 (GRC, Quantico, VA), sec 2, chap 6, p. 41.

impossible to avoid civilian casualties.[117] One tank was struck with a round from a recoilless rifle and instantly caught fire. One of the greatest threats to any tank, the rifle is designed to pierce armor, and a well-aimed shot in the engine compartment, like this one, could take a tank down. As the crew tried to put out the fire, up to 250 Iraqi soldiers tried to capitalize on the situation. While boarding another vehicle, one soldier was shot in the eye, and others barely made it out alive. Trucks loaded with Iraqi soldiers arrived on the scene, and the convoy ripped them to pieces as they dismounted. Leaving the tank after much delay, the convoy pressed on, crushing concrete barriers that the Iraqis hastily put in place to stop them.

Task Force 1-64 AR linked up with friendly forces at Baghdad International Airport and ended the first thunder run. Soldiers afterward gaped at their shot-up tanks and wondered how they got out alive. The commander of 1-64, Lieutenant Colonel Eric Schwartz, stated in an interview,

> I was emotionally spent. One of my tank commanders had been killed. I had a soldier shot in the eye, shot in the forehead, shot in the shoulder, shot in the back, shot in the face . . . I just needed time for myself, and one of the other battalion commanders from 1st Brigade came over and didn't say a single word. He asked me, "Are you okay?" And I said, "I don't know." He looked at me and then turned around and walked away, and that was the best thing he could have done.[118]

On April 7, at 0600, the Army conducted another thunder run directly toward Baghdad's city center. The Iraqi reaction to the first thrust was not a sophisticated, concerted effort by any means,

---

117 Fontenot, *On Point*, 344.
118 Lieutenant Colonel Eric Schwartz, interview, 18 May 2003, from Fonteneot, *On point*, 346.

prompting the coalition command to make another, bolder strike into Baghdad. Again heading north on Highway 8, this time there was a slew of mines in the road. Captain David Hibner with Company D, 10th Engineers recalled the events of the early morning.

> This was the mission and everyone was counting on us. This was it, the attack on Baghdad. We were going in first and had to clear the way for the rest of the troops. If we couldn't get the minefield breached, it wasn't going to happen, so we made the decision to pick up the mines with our hands as fast as we could.[119]

Moving them by hand, a lane was quickly cleared, and the column began receiving fire.

> An RPG hit one of my vehicles. It was just to the left of me. They got us. I could feel the blast and feel the heat. The vehicle that was hit drifted off course and I thought the worst, that everyone inside was dead. But they were just knocked out; they came to and went right back in formation. The RPG didn't penetrate the vehicle because we put so much crap on the outside of our vehicles as we could. Rucksacks, MRE boxes, tents, if it could be strapped to the outside, we did it, because it gets the RPGs to detonate early and it ruins the blast effect. The whole front of the vehicle had peeled off, as if God had come down and slapped everything off the front of it. It was gone, splattered everywhere, pitted and burned. As we were driving along, we could see underwear and trousers spilling out of the rucksacks that had holes in them. But that's a small price to pay for the hit we took.[120]

---
119 Captain David Hibner in Larson, Chuck, *Heroes Among Us*, 138.
120 Hibner in Larson, *Heroes*, 139.

The column bypassed many obstacles the Iraqis placed in the way until they came upon the tank that had been disabled by the recoilless rifle days before. The Iraqis were in the process of stripping it, and the column decimated the scavengers. The fighting was fierce, as the Iraqis were better prepared this time, but the brigade kept moving through the fire and passed under the famous crossed swords in central Baghdad, next seizing the park and monument complex and the Tomb of the Unknown Soldier. Captain Hibner recalled the chaos on the ground.

> I think the enemy realized they couldn't hurt us when we were on the move so they waited until we stopped. Then we started getting fire from everywhere. I was standing outside when the first mortar round landed. I had a media team with me. The mortar landed nearby and I'm surprised none of us got hurt. Everybody scrambled into the vehicles, and the mortars fell continually from that moment on. They never stopped.[121]

Small arms fire poured into the brigade even as the brigade commander planted its flag in the square. The brigade was there to stay, leaving the tanks downtown, destroying the morale of the Iraqi resistance, yet the east had not been taken; that would fall to the Marines. The fight for Baghdad was not over.

Perhaps the best part for all of us was the order to shed our chemical suits. I remember well stripping off the smelly NBC charcoal-lined suit. Our bodies could breathe again. The sunlight hit our desert uniforms for the first time in in weeks and cooked the salt within the fabric; motivation soared. Here we were, just north of Baghdad, saying, "Thank God" as we removed the protective shells and tossed them into a pile. Apparently, command believed the

---

[121] Ibid., 139.

threat of an NBC attack was gone; even Saddam not crazy enough to use them within city limits.

The Marines from each RCT moved out early on April 9 to seize objectives on the eastern half of Baghdad, which included paramilitary bases, secret police headquarters, Baghdad University, and Saddam's presidential palace. Intelligence on the enemy within the city was nearly nonexistent. Irregular formations had been spotted by reconnaissance and reports from the Army in the west stated the same thing, but exactly where they were was a mystery outside the university. The CIA reported that the Fedayeen had chosen that spot to make a stand. Outside that meager piece of information, Baghdad was a mystery to us, especially those on the ground who didn't have the advantage of the latest information.

RCT-5 attacked in the city, ready for a fight with a "thunder run" of their own. As to the division's main effort, no one knew what would happen, but the tanks up front faced stiff resistance a few kilometers into the city just like the Army had. Iraqis used small arms liberally, spraying the tanks that rode past them. Tankers buttoned up inside heard rounds clanking on the hull, which was relatively safe except from RPGs. From alleyways and rooftops they came, miraculously missing or bouncing off the uranium armor. Two A-10 Warthogs circled overhead, opening up their 30 mm rotary cannon on command from the tanks on the ground, taking out enemy positions the tanks had missed on their way. Most of the fighters had shed their uniforms, and it was difficult to distinguish them from civilians. With the palace in view, one tank was hit when several RPG teams opened up, wounding two Marines within. One tank out of action, and bullets flying everywhere, Alpha Company surrounded that palace at the very heart of Baghdad and held its ground.[122] At least 100 Fedayeen lay dead in the streets.

RCT-7 assaulted from the southeast to the northwest, claiming the Ministry of Intelligence, the Ministry of Oil, the Iraqi Air Force

---

122   2nd Tank Battalion Command Chronology, 13.

headquarters, Uday Hussein's offices, and the already bombed Fedayeen headquarters. While they were claiming most of the east side, 3rd Battalion, 4th Marines rolled into Firdos Square in downtown Baghdad, which was dominated by a huge statue of Saddam. Reporters from the nearby Palestine Hotel came to see the scene, which unfolded as one of the greatest moments of the entire war—indeed, in history itself. An M-88 Hercules of 1st Tank Battalion hoisted its crane, and a Marine, Corporal Edward Chin, at its apex produced contraband, an American flag, and draped Saddam's cold face with it as the crowd watched. It was probably the first American flag Baghdad had yet seen as we were all under strict orders to hide them. Command had the benefit of watching the live stream of the occasion, and, appalled at the audacity of the American flag being produced, the order was given to remove it and replace it with an Iraqi flag that a civilian just happened to be carrying. A cable was wrapped around the six-meter-high statue in quick order, and to everyone's joy, the Hercules pulled down the monument; it crashed down in front of a crowd of cheering civilians, its head decapitated and dragged off to be chopped into pieces.

It is an image that will live forever in history—an iconic moment that defined the struggle. The entire world watched the moment over and over. It was a glorious exclamation point of Operation Iraqi Freedom. It symbolized the fall of a regime and the beginning of a new government, a new story for Iraq. A Rebirth. It was a bold idea hatched by Marines in the center of Baghdad, no doubt by enlisted men, who dominate the ranks of any professional military. It was, as Winston Churchill once stated, their finest hour. The fighting, however, was not over. Just to the east, and indeed all around them, Marines were bogged down in urban combat, and the alleyways and boulevards were lit up; the expended brass casings made the streets look as if they were paved with gold.

There was trouble at Baghdad University; 1st Battalion, 7th Marines had finally engaged the Fedayeen the CIA warned them about.

Steady small arms and RPG fire came from within, and the Marines crouched on the outside perimeter for protection. The university was lined with a concrete wall that kept the Marines safe for the moment. An amtrack backed up and, coming at full speed, rammed the wall several times until it capitulated in several feet of rubble. It then rushed the opening and the infantry spilled in. Multiple military vehicles were inside, mostly pickup trucks with mounted machine guns, and, under the command of a lone corporal, one after another was pummeled with the combined power of a platoon of M-16s. Bunkers lay in the distance, and the unnamed corporal directed the fire into each of them, silencing the occupants. Before long, one of the bunkers exploded as the Marines hit an ammunition cache. The university, a place of learning, was now a place of war. The news crews ate up the action in real time, and the Fedayeen were killed in quick succession; the whole complex seemed ablaze with destruction.[123]

From the back of a seven-ton truck, with other displaced Marines who had lost their tanks on the way, I viewed Baghdad from behind a rifle pointed to the rooftops and alleyways, looking for snipers and opportunists. Right behind the amtracks, over the rickety bridges hastily constructed by daring crews under fire, the Diyala passed behind me, and the city with its dull, earthy colors loomed all around. It was overwhelming. Until that time, I, like all the other Marines, had fought on the highways and outskirts of civilization, and suddenly we were surrounded by three, four, and five-story buildings that could easily harbor the enemy. And he was there.

The occasional pop ruptured ears and the metal of the truck or the flap of canvas peppered with holes. People looked up from their daily routine and mouths gaped. People filed onto balconies and looked down on the Americans, who stared right back at them. Children playing ball and running in the streets stopped completely and waved frantically with smiling faces. They had no idea we were coming. The information minister had done his work well. The Iraqis

---

123   West, *The March Up*, 229.

filed out of their homes among the chaos and waved us on. They had no idea the danger they were in, and what kind of stress they put on our shoulders to take extra care to discern targets before firing. But they were there, giving us thumbs-up and approaching so close to the tanks that they could have touched us.

The liberation outside was stifled for us because we had endured an exhaustive road march that left RCT-5 parched inside tanks and tracked vehicles. The average tanker had bathed in his own sweat for weeks, his socks were slimy in his boots, and the heat inside the tank dulled the moment outside, which was unfolding as one of the greatest liberations in history. From the mud-brick homes to the many triple-story apartments, we peered out of hatches, rifles at the ready, the whine of our turbine engines blotting out the cheers of the people. Less tactical minds were influenced by the people's commotion, but the most sharp and high-strung looked to the rooftops, to the small alleyways hiding enemy tanks, and even to the children playing with enemy gear found in the street.

I was on edge. I had not slept well since enduring the combat march, and I caught myself more than once pouring out my seat, bearing my weapon down on someone I thought was a threat. I scared the hell out of a few Iraqis, but they recovered from their shock and continued cheering and peddling their wares: bitter alcohol, even worse cigarettes, and military souvenirs for the chance to make off with US dollars. Few of us, therefore, appreciated what was happening—what we accomplished since leaving Kuwait mere weeks earlier. All we could think of was the next hot meal, the next cold shower, and lust over the photos of women plastered within our tanks, for those who still had tanks; some of the women were respectable, those you wrote home to Mom about, but most were not.

Within earshot of the chaos at the university, some Marines got the idea to throw rations to the crowd; some, with humor, threw their unused pork-chop dinners to the unsuspecting Muslims, who gobbled the contraband. Other Marines produced candy, and the skinny Iraqi children fought one another for it in the street. It was a parade interrupted by short periods of terror when we spotted an enemy bunker and riddled it with chaos and fire. Terror when a brave Fedayeen chose to shoot at us from the rooftops, right over the heads of their peaceful countrymen. All of these things kept us guessing—sitting ducks with the capital looming all around.

Word came on the radio and rumor quickly spread that young Iraqi daughters were being hoisted up by their fathers to Marines in the convoy, pleading for one of us to take them to America. What could the Marines do at such a request? How it resonated, though, that fathers would give up their children instead of being with them in Iraq. That life here was so terrible and that they loved their children so much as to put them in the hands of a total stranger and never see them again. How little we knew, how little we grasped the desperation of the Iraqi until he offered us his daughters. It broke one's heart having to say no. Marines who experienced it understood the reality of life in Iraq, if only for a moment, and in an instant that father and the daughter faded into the dust the tanks produced—a searing memory I thanked God I could only imagine.

The parade progressed, and one of the young Iraqi ladies covered from head to toe in a burka spotted one of the handsome Marines in my company and was so moved by his rugged features that she unsnapped the shawl covering her face, and in full view of God and countrymen showed her face to him. Overcome by the sacrilege of the moment, the mother of the girl pushed her way through the crowd, and, coming upon her, beat the daylights out of her for daring to show her affections to the American. There was nothing we could do; for most of us it was the first real instance of culture shock. The black-clad abuser and child faded behind us, leaving us thankful to be Americans.

I was surprised to see civilians with hordes of goods pass the column, trucks and pony-drawn wagons loaded down to maximum capacity. The plundering Iraqis didn't seem to care we were there. I couldn't believe my eyes at the glimpse of an old woman, no more than four and a half feet tall, perfectly balancing a refrigerator on her head, walking normally and able to bring herself to a jog. Iraqis swarmed government storehouses in plain view of the convoy because the Iraqi police discarded their uniforms for fear of being shot, and therefore discarded their duties. There was no law for the moment. An oppressed people for the first time in their lives could take what they wanted without repercussion, and by the look on their faces they relished every minute of it.

The Army and Marines in their respective quadrants of the city were doing their best to secure the streets. After Baghdad officially fell on April 13, troops had new problems to deal with, such as establishing semipermanent bases, maintaining security, and dealing with the shaken populace. The US government contracted to rebuild Iraq, repairing calamities like damaged water lines and power plants, and rehabilitating 1,200 schools[124] almost immediately. An American-owned corporation called Bechtel enjoyed a billion-dollar contract agreed to not a week after the war's end and likely to continue for years to come in subsequent occupation.[125]

There was a good reason for the hasty government spending. The situation in Iraq was vastly deteriorating. Looters hit department stores as the heavy cavalry moved in; government buildings and even hospitals fell victim, and it was obvious to the US troops patrolling the streets. There was little to nothing one could do to stop looters besides chase them away or detain them because there were virtually no reliable police, and the language barrier between gulf-arabic and english caused much confusion on the ground, even with interpreters.

Amid the mob and busy Americans, a well-coordinated sack of the Baghdad Museum was quietly underway. The guards and curators had fled. The precision attack was carried out as if the criminals had

---
124 Bechtel Corporation, *Images of Iraq*, Company Archives, http://www.bechtel.com/images_of_iraq.html
125 John Perkins, Confessions of an *Economic Hit Man*, (New York: Penguin, 2006), 251-53.

a shopping list, smashing displays and carrying off Iraq's national treasures, such as a heavy statue of King Argon II, and the "Mona Lisa of Mesopotamia," the famous Lady of Warka from 3100 BC. Fifteen thousand artifacts were stolen, most being small items that fit in a pocket. It is common for looting to take place amid the chaos of war, but the rape of the Baghdad Museum was outrageous, even though many knew what was going on. When asked about the museum, Donald Rumsfeld exclaimed with an air of virtue,

> Stuff happens, it is untidy, and freedom is untidy, and free people are free to make mistakes, and commit crimes, and do bad things. They are also free to live their lives and do wonderful things, and that's what's going to happen here.

All happening a stone's throw from me, it was obvious that Baghdad had been taken, and the people were truly free. Our leadership neglected to give us instruction on how to regain control of the fractured city. People were everywhere. The citizenry jumped over bodies in the street to jack a car, crack a safe, or cheer on the Americans. Marines are not trained to be an occupational force—they are an invading force. We had no idea what to do besides secure the ground we stood on, and that's exactly what we did.

Stepping onto the ground numb and accustomed to pain, I stared at Baghdad University, made of tan brick like the rest of the city. It looked like any campus in the US, but it was built more conservatively, closer together so as to not hoard space. A few small dorms hugged the property, small gardens and civilian vehicles leaving it the energy of having been just recently occupied, with the simmering military vehicles the Marines destroyed off in the distance. I was surprised to see scud launchers next to the university with rockets still attached. There were two of these. Trucks with spilled military supplies abounded—not a sign of students anywhere.

My platoon sergeant immediately took charge of the area, posting security, and the tankers who had just been in combat stopped to rest in the shade of palm trees within the courtyard. I sat in the shade collecting my thoughts, wired up while the rest of the Marines took shots at everything and anything that looked suspicious outside the university gate. I wrote in my journal, spoke to a few friends, and was glad in the knowledge that Baghdad was taken.

It wasn't long, however, before I got antsy as the commotion at the university had not died down, and I sought to employ myself using my rank to round up a couple of Marines to patrol the area. I noticed that the university door was open and decided to explore. With the tanks outside and the few Fedayeen that defended the university dead, I thought it safe enough to browse the corridors. My boots crunched as I stepped inside. Shattered glass and objects lay strewn across the floors—a nightmare of overturned tables, papers and textbooks. The Marines with me veered off in different directions, shouting "clear" in every successive room they entered, but it soon became obvious that such caution was not needed as the occupants were dead. A gymnastics teacher's office blanketed with medals and trophies, whistles, and stopwatches greeted me. Next to it was the dean's office, which interested all of the Marines. The room had the smell of expensive cologne and a desk littered with administrative papers, tea cups of surprisingly fine quality, and file cabinets that begged to be opened. Needles were on the desk, along with small red vials filled with some attractive liquid. It was a royal mess, and we concluded that the fluid was the "dope" that the jihadists used to hop themselves up on. Many of these things were carried off by Marines.

Through another doorway, I moved into an artist's room, tinted orange due to the light beaming from behind ginger draperies. A soft carpet welcomed me—I had not slept on something so soft in months. Small tables lay precariously around the room, with the artists' palette and oil paints upon them. The students had left their paintings. There must have been over thirty of them and, from their appearance and quality, were created by those my age or younger. I saw spinning wheels, clay pots, the clay sometimes still wet, and a breathtaking picture of a brunette woman with piercing blue eyes challenged me not to covet. I found pencil drawings of Saddam depicting him as if he were a savior. The reverence for this man was astounding. Even if it was fake reverence, with his picture on every wall, this man had some leadership qualities, even if only incurring fear. Having been in power since 1979 through wanton intimidation and murder, it made sense the people would fear acting any way else.

I passed through dim hallways quietly, the first time I had been alone in months. Papers blew across the floor, the breeze carrying the voices of my comrades, excited and enthusiastic over their finds; orange curtains grazing my uniform, I walked slowly, coming upon a sight indeed. I beheld a huge mural depicting Saddam with his patriotic flag surrounded by little children. All the children were focused on Saddam; an AK-47 rested in a child's hands with a rainbow parting the clouds behind. It felt like patriotism, but in reality it was fear, lies—an otherwise extraordinary painting made to appease, no doubt, the secret police and the Fedayeen that had just died in that very building. Dying for Saddam. Dying for nothing.

Moving on, it was my turn to covet. The library. Under normal circumstances, the books would not have interested me since I didn't know arabic. However, it turned out that this college taught extensive english, and exactly half of the library's contents were in my native tongue. Glancing across the abandoned checkout desk, my eye caught a short statue around eighteen inches tall covered in a black pigment. An artifact. The head was classical ancient Sumerian, her gorgeous hair knotted up in a whirl, empty eyes glaring absently. She sat on a plinth with no features on her smooth dress—a work of genius. Past the knees I saw, to my amazement, cuneiform lettering. The familiar notched symbols flowed down the front of her knees.

There were others in the sunlit room. A smaller green one in the corner of the library, a woman with faded features behind glass, balancing a pot on her head. She also bore the lettering, tempting me as well. A statue of an Assyrian bull the size of a fist, which could easily have been pocketed, was in another corner; I resisted the urge. I paused and listened to gunfire outside the university; it was time to go. Before I left, I removed the heavy glass containing the black statue and picked up the polished, lidless figure.

Iraq. So long as I was attached to the American military machine, I would never truly understand her. As fragile as the ancient woman in my hands, she rested in America's hands. She rested on the goodness of officers and enlisted men; American democracy. I placed her as I found her; it would be up to America to do the same, shielding Iraq from harm. I replaced the glass and left.

CHAPTER IX

Home

I PLACED THE PORCELAIN on its saucer, grasped the warm spoon resting in the hot Earl Grey tea, and began to stir. My civilian clothes fit loosely on my 150-pound frame and seemed incomplete without the snug fit of a gas mask carrier around the waist. Home. Camp Lejeune, North Carolina. I look up from my dinner to the blaring television. More of our men ambushed and killed last night, occupying the same town where the midnight mortars hit my unit, Ad Diwaniyah. *More are yet to come,* I wrote in my journal. I was blessed with time. Whereas before I could hardly jot my thoughts down, I now wrote all I could:

> Terrorism is an idea. In history at least, it is impossible to suppress what dwells in the minds of men. Iraq will turn into the next regular duty station for every branch of our armed forces. Although we did the service of ridding a people from oppression, a growing opposition towards the US forces lingers. Already the post-war casualties outnumber those

lost in the official war, and will continue to climb up until the very day America withdraws from Iraq.[126]

Between March 19 when the invasion began and April 30, the span of forty-two days, only 109 Americans were killed with an additional 542 wounded, making Operation Iraqi Freedom one of the least deadly conflicts in American history. On the Iraqi side, an estimated 9,200 combatants were killed with 3,750 noncombatants during the invasion phase, which President Bush declared over May 1. Against a nation that boasted seventeen regular army divisions and six Republican Guard divisions totaling about 350,000 troops, it is simply amazing that the US saw so few casualties.[127] As for Iraq, and those poor citizens who were caught in the crossfire, I wondered if any in that number were because of me or other Marines that were with me on March 27. I might never know.

Sipping my tea, I heard "breaking" news that Mr. Hussein's sons, Ouday and Husay, had just been killed. It was finally official. Having left that dismal place, I sat in my chair and listened to news I thought had already occurred. The bodies, loaded with bullets, were on public display for the first time in Baghdad. The US government needed to supply the newspapers and TV networks with ever more victories, and this news was a whopper. In the months after the war, nothing had been accomplished save a large number of casualties. *Why not inform the press of the siblings' death when America began to question exactly what we're still doing in Iraq? Keep the motivation high*, I thought.

Out in town, a civilian approached me. "Did you just get back?"

I replied, "Yes."

"Well, we shouldn't have ever been over there," he said matter-of-factly.

The statement struck me. I had not planned an answer, and in that moment I had to create my own apologetics. Iraq was a war many

---

126 Grant, Journal, March 23, 2003–December 21, 2005, 54.
127 Hosmer, *Why the Iraqi*, 1-2.

thought unjust—a war for oil interest, a war fabricated against an innocent people without the proof of WMDs that propelled us there. Those very thoughts plagued me even as my boots were on the ground, doing my duty. To justify the war, especially afterwards when every Iraq War veteran had been informed that the war was unjust, the veteran had to fight for the right to have his war viewed in honorable terms—convincing everyone who challenged him that what he did was good and worthy of remembrance. It's sad for a warrior to fight when the civilians he fights for know nothing of military matters and challenge him, calling him a warmonger even though all he did was serve his country.

Thinking quickly, I replied, "Well, if there's blood on the streets, someone's got to hang."

It was a terrible reply, but when critically examined, it was true. What did the world expect the United States to do short of taking drastic military action against evil regimes? If America did nothing after 9/11, terrorism would have been sanctioned by inaction. We learned the hard way what Athenagoras of Syracuse said thousands of years ago: "If a man does not strike first, he will be the first struck." Taking Baghdad sent a message: that the US would act against dangerous volatile governments who threatened our security and the security of peaceful nations abroad.

It was all I could do to shake the civilian's hand as he thanked me for my service.

There is a sharp military-civilian divide in many nations, not just in America. Civilians send their sons and daughters away, and they come back changed, full of jargon and habits that those whom the soldier calls "civilians" don't get. The military man becomes altogether another creature with a new circle of friends and associates that divide his old life from the new. It is difficult for anyone to understand what they have not experienced, and civilians, grateful for the service and sacrifice of their sons and daughters, reach out in any way they can to relate to the military yoke.

One thing that stands out in common between the military and the civilian is humanity. Most who are Christian understand John 15:13: "Greater love hath no man than this: that he lay down his life for his friends." Blot out the training, how a military man is made, take out the desire for glory, and what remains is duty, honor, and compassion, traits that civilian fathers and mothers instill in their children that the military waxed in their lives. These offspring will march in Veterans Day parades, perform Memorial Day services, and stand honor guard for fallen veterans. Everyone appreciates veterans and their outward displays of commitment to God and country. "Thank you for your service" is often the highest praise the civilian can give to their sons and daughters, and it is often their greatest understanding of the military man.

★ ★ ★ ★ ★

Back on base, Marines abused alcohol, reclaiming their bodies from the massive detox that was Iraq. I was no different. Others found peace in simpler things like books or chatting on the phone with girlfriends. Some simply vanished home or were never quite the same. Close friends who stayed behind greeted me, and before long I caught myself avoiding them, doing anything just to get away, like running off into the woods where I first said my prayer. I was still in Iraq. Indeed, I wanted to go back because everything was simpler there—black and white. I would never get my chance. It felt like just yesterday that I had I watched the eyes of wives, families, and children flood with tears at their warriors' return. Each warrior smiled and held those frightening moments behind their eyes with a lock and key, seldom to be revealed yet defining every movement.

America was different now. No—I was different. Not long after returning, I began to forget Iraq, everything I had done, and for years tried to resume a normal life. It wasn't just me struggling to acclimate; all Marines were doing the same. I would only remain in the Corps for another year, and it was a year of hard work, a year of maturity, and a year of forgetting.

I put away my journals until something happened to me that caused me to open them again, sand within the pages I read and remembered, and in that lonely cabin in the woods I faced my greatest challenge. Greater than the Fedayeen, greater than jihadists, the greatest I had ever faced, and it would either kill me or bring me lasting peace. A struggle that is very much alive as I write this. No. The story is not over.

EPILOGUE

My Time in
the Woods

All men dream, but not equally. Those who dream by night in the dusty recesses of their minds wake up in the day to find it was vanity, but the dreamers of the day are dangerous men, for they may act their dreams with open eyes, to make it possible.

T. E. LAWRENCE

AFTER THE WAR I saw the most extraordinary thing in my barracks room. I had been dreaming and was startled awake; something was staring at me. Widening my eyes, I blinked hard. Ripping off my sheets, I curled into a fetal position on the adjacent concrete wall; the cold touch reminded me I was awake.

This was real.

In the darkness, a dim figure sat in a chair facing my bed.

I blinked again.

"Who are you? What do you want?" The figure was motionless. A small girl. She had curly black hair that fell about a white dress with blue trim. I hadn't the time to be frightened while my eyes focused on her tiny dangling feet. Magnetism filled the space between us—a numbness closer and more intimate than I had ever known. My eyes fixed upon the one place I could have found explanation, seeking a mouth, a word or message to set my nerves at ease. Looking, I found nothing but a blackness deeper than the dark room around me.

She had no face.

Seconds passed before I crept slowly forward, eyes locked on the visitor like I was in the presence of some predator. She remained unmoving with hands clasped across her lap peacefully, and by her demeanor she, or it, meant me no harm.

My roommate lay across the barracks room in a deep sleep. He needed to see this; I needed him to be awake. My voice left me; in any other circumstance I would have used it. There was something about the girl that stuck inside. The blackness of that face subdued me.

Grasping a boot and raising it to throw, I scrambled up with force enough to crash back against the wall. I dropped the boot. There was no more need to throw it at my roommate. She was gone.

Not long after I saw her, I returned home to New York State. I had grand plans to buy a log cabin in the woods to get away; four years of the Marine Corps and war offended me. I wanted nothing more than to forget what I had done and live my days out in peace and stillness. I walked up to the cabin with my key in hand and regarded the beauty of the emerald woods; Honeoye Lake in the distance comforted me. This was it. I was home.

I lost impetus to rise in rank in the Corps and accepted an honorable discharge instead. I hung my NCO sword on the wall with pleasure. It was over, a chapter of my life ended, and thank God I had lived to see it. The only ambition I had was to whip my decrepit house into shape, and I went about my business alone with only my cat to keep me company and the occasional visit from my parents and family.

I wanted to forget, and I set about forgetting. Every day I drank a half bottle of whisky. I knew it wasn't normal, but I didn't care. I took long walks into the emerald forest for hours on end, sometimes drunk, sometimes not, but always returned to the cabin in one piece. I stayed up late drinking and thinking of nothing, just staring at the ceiling with my beloved cat nuzzling me. Alone. I didn't mind the quiet. I had been surrounded by Marines, noise, and gunfire so long that all I wanted was to lie there and embrace a cloudless mind, and what a joy it was to be filled with nothing but the rudimentary. My thoughts were kept general, and for precious little time I had everything I wanted.

Have Another

And why not?
I've been across the world and back,
 was nearly killed many times.
The bullets whizzing and the mortars dropping all over me.
What does it make a difference if I take another shot?
 I am after all, safe
My brow is heavy as I drop it back,
 Oh the days I have seen
  I end up on the floor, helpless
This is how I kill it, this is what he wants
 My silence, my gifts mute,
Locked up in a cabin away from the world
 Oh the battles I have won.
  I was once a prince living forever
   Everything goes black,
I can almost feel his warm hand.

Then I saw her again. Alone at my cabin, I saw her staring through my window and I froze. *No. What?*

"What the hell?"

She disappeared and left me with the same disorientation as when I saw her before. What was she? A ghost? She couldn't be real, but it sure felt real. My hands were sweating and my eyes bulging. I drank and tried to forget the faceless being, but soon she became an everyday occurrence in person and in thought, and I began to wonder why I was seeing her and feeling her presence as she swung around a corner or walked down the woodland trails with me. I began to talk to her even if I didn't see her; she never spoke back. She was always with me before long—while I was chopping wood, changing my oil, painting the walls, or shooting targets out back. Everywhere. After a while I didn't mind her, and it was that comfort that drove me to seek help.

Considering it madness, I sought the help of a psychologist at a VA hospital. My palms moistened as I told him where I had been and what I was seeing, and in short time he gave me a diagnosis. I had PTSD, post-traumatic stress disorder. The girl I was seeing was some sort of manifestation of my time in Iraq, and I needed therapy.

This was not how it was supposed to be. That part of my life was over, and I didn't want to go back. All I wanted to do was sit and forget—take my walks in the woods and forget. I had to find the courage to fight as I once did the Fedayeen, but instead of fighting an enemy that I could wound or shoot and kill, I had to fight myself, that mighty fortress that didn't allow anyone in and divulged no secrets. I was not sure if I could win, and that terrified me.

Post-Traumatic Stress Disorder

Leave me alone.

Let me sit.

I have been to places you cannot imagine.

    Everyday,

I have to deal with you, and sometimes, it's all I can do to smile.

You are a co-worker, a wife, husband, brother, sister and

    You know me.

So give me a minute. Let me sit. And, if I stare blankly, don't worry,

I am in the desert somewhere eating a memory, stabbing at an enemy.

    So you can sleep safe at night.

She was linked to that terrible event on March 27, 2003. I never knew for sure if any civilians had been killed that day, but the gut-wrenching feeling I had was that they were, and no matter how much therapy I had, I could not shake the terrible feeling that innocent lives had been lost. The girl appeared to me on occasion but with less frequency than she once had, so I knew the therapy was working. At some point, however, I set in motion a plan to rid myself of the ghostly image once and for all, and that plan was to *return to Iraq*, to the mud-brick homes, and find out for myself if any civilians died that day. My plans were great. I bought Arab clothes, started learning Gulf Arabic, bought Iraqi dinars, and learned to live life like I would not return to America, as if I was going to die in the pursuit; otherwise, I cheapened the value of my life and God's blessing that I was still living it. I was alive for a reason, and I truly believed that returning to Iraq was the reason—to ask forgiveness for my actions under fire that day.

At night I had dreams that startled me awake. One night I drafted this poem knowing the dream I had was of me in Iraq, shivering in the darkness.

Alone in Iraq

In a dream
I had once,
I saw the night sky so foreign to me. The stars bent over a streak of dawn.
I felt peace though I knew it to be the other side of the world.
When I looked
   Up
   At the stars so re-arraigned from the fields of home;
      Somehow,
I regarded it as the same. A same likeness.
And, at a certain moment, I think,
   They began to fall on me in force. In unison,
A deadly host of heaven combined in aim to my glistening eyes.
I didn't mind.
      Here it is, the end of my days....is this how it feels to have walked the earth without
      Listening
      To the calling of my heart?
         I now stand unfinished. For now I wish I had listened

Thank God it was just a dream.

★ ★ ★ ★ ★

My plans brought me back to the Marine Corps, as I considered it expedient to my goal. In 2006 I volunteered to return to the ranks. I lifted my sword off the wall and sheathed it. I was a Marine again, and no one knew that I was really going back to return to Iraq; that was my secret. I packed my bags and left the cabin; I left the woods, my solitude, behind forever. With sadness I left to Camp Pendleton, California, to serve as a sergeant. I had no idea that my orders would change my life and lead to a great understanding of troops in combat.

I served on the Haditha and Hamdania trials. I was an escort chauffeuring the media to military court where Marines and sailors were being brought up on charges of murder. In Haditha, Iraq, on

November 19, 2005, a platoon of Marines was engaged in a firefight after one of their Humvees was destroyed by a roadside bomb. One of their comrades died instantly in the explosion, and they were engaged by small arms fire from both sides of the road. Confused and full of adrenaline, the Marines ran to the nearby homes and threw in grenades and entered the homes where Iraqi civilians were hiding. What followed was the alleged civilian massacre.

The news spread like wildfire, and it was up to me and a handful of Marines at Camp Pendleton to oblige the media and allow them into the military tribunal. I sat in the courtroom and heard the accused's bloody stories and felt for their confusion; I was in their shoes in 2003, though I told no one. I took notes in the back of the courtroom daily to try to figure out what was going on in the Marines' heads to make them fire upon civilians. The knowledge I gained was simple—the Marines were engaged the moment their Humvee was destroyed, just as I was engaged the moment bullets impacted all around me in Hells Wrecker. We fought for our lives; we fought to survive against an enemy who used civilians for cover. That was their decision; not our fault that civilians had been killed. I still, however, wanted to know.

All the while, I had my demons, keeping quiet, reading books on Iraq, and finding quotes like this one from Kate J. Tate, dear to my heart: "Recovering from PTSD is being fragile and strong at the same time. It is a beautiful medley of constantly being broken down and pieced together. I am a painting almost done to completion, beautiful, but not quite complete."

In contrast was the incident at Hamdania, Iraq, in April 26, 2006. An Iraqi civilian, Hashim Ibrahim Awad, was taken from his home in the middle of the night by a squad of angry Marines. They knew he had harbored insurgents and provided them aid, but they had no proof. They forced him into a ditch with a shovel as if he were planting an IED and shot him numerous times until he died. The Marines were arraigned and tried at Camp Pendleton, and I sat in the back of the courtroom listening to their story. I felt their frustration knowing that the civilian was plotting to harm them and their superiors told them there was nothing they could do about it. Limited warfare at its finest. I had no doubt that Awad was guilty of harboring insurgents, but the way the Marines went about killing him was wrong. One could make an argument that they were being engaged daily by Awad and other insurgents and that they were in combat all along. The Hamdania incident proved to me that, along with Haditha, total war was not compatible with the American psyche.

When it came down to it, the Marines should not have been tried unless tried by a judge and prosecutor who had been to combat themselves. Regardless, it struck me that I could be in these men's shoes if I told my story. So, it gave me all the more reason to keep quiet. I kept planning to go to Iraq in any way I could imagine, either with the Marines or by myself, and in the midst of all the trials, an unexpected thing happened. I fell in love.

I met my wife at a seaside bonfire near the pier in Oceanside, California, and all my plans were put on hold. She had a daughter, six years old, and I immediately bonded with her. She was life, whereas the image I had been seeing was hollow and magnetic. Her little daughter worked her way into my heart, and I began to forget all my plans for Iraq, where I most likely would have died. Suddenly I had something to live for. This was the reason God preserved me; I knew it in my soul. If there were civilians dead as a result of combat action that day in March long ago, they were the fault of the Fedayeen who sacrificed them mercilessly for nothing. That's what I told myself.

The ghostly little girl disappeared. I have not seen her in years. She left, and I began to heal. I returned to the cabin in the woods with my new family, to that place of forgetting, and it became a place of healing. With my sword remounted on the wall, I could truly close a chapter in my life. However, it is impossible to think that the war didn't change me. It still dictates how I interact with people, how I view the world, and how I view my children as they sleep at night. I used to think that I did not have a right to children because I was capable of such terrible things. God has proved me otherwise, patching up my feelings with overwhelming love for others to silence the dark one, his demons that constantly try me.

So, we come to this book. I write for my children as much as I do the veteran. Learn from my experiences and know that, through God, there is peace for you. PTSD is nothing against such a terrific force. There is nothing you can't overcome. Take heart, for you are stronger than you think. Take the fight to the corridors of your own mind and know that you are not alone. Take comfort, my brothers, for God has a Purpose for your life.

> *He that masters his own soul is greater than he that can conquer a city.*
> **INSPIRED BY PROVERBS 16:32**

God's purpose. Something inside my soul cries to return to Iraq. If I could do it again, I would have leapt off the M-88 and charged the Fedayeen. At least then I would know what happened, even if it killed me. I would have closed my eyes on the world knowing, instead of the daily uncertainty that cripples me, urging me to return. A terrifying pursuit as I have children that love me, a wife that loves me, and a community that loves me, a God that loves me. Look in my eyes and you will see it there, a man who could have it all if only he knew what happened that day.

A day may come that I go, returning to the mud-brick homes, putting to rest my heart as God has forgiven me. But it is human forgiveness I seek, to make peace with my brother as I am commanded in Matthew 5:24. What I need is in the desert, a tangible hand on mine to release me whether any died that day or not. A human touch; human grace. A single word to set a soul free. Whatever happens—*to* God or *with* God in the desert—I say with a clear conscience, "There by the Grace of God go I."

No. The story is not over.

Going Back

Somewhere in the back of my soul it has been hiding
    Beneath the rudimentary – the foundation of a great sin
That somehow, some way, I must return to that place
        where time stopped
Back to Iraq in that cluster of mud huts where it all began.
Somehow I must go there to find out what happened because guilt
    Cripples me.
It is the foundation of my maturity, the origin of a great sin which I may be
able to lie to rest with
        a little questioning.
In my dreams I approach the hut and see a dim figure there
    He says:
        "Welcome brother."
We then go in for tea and lamb and talk of the days before the war,
    Before fate connected our lives forever.

Littera Scripta Manet

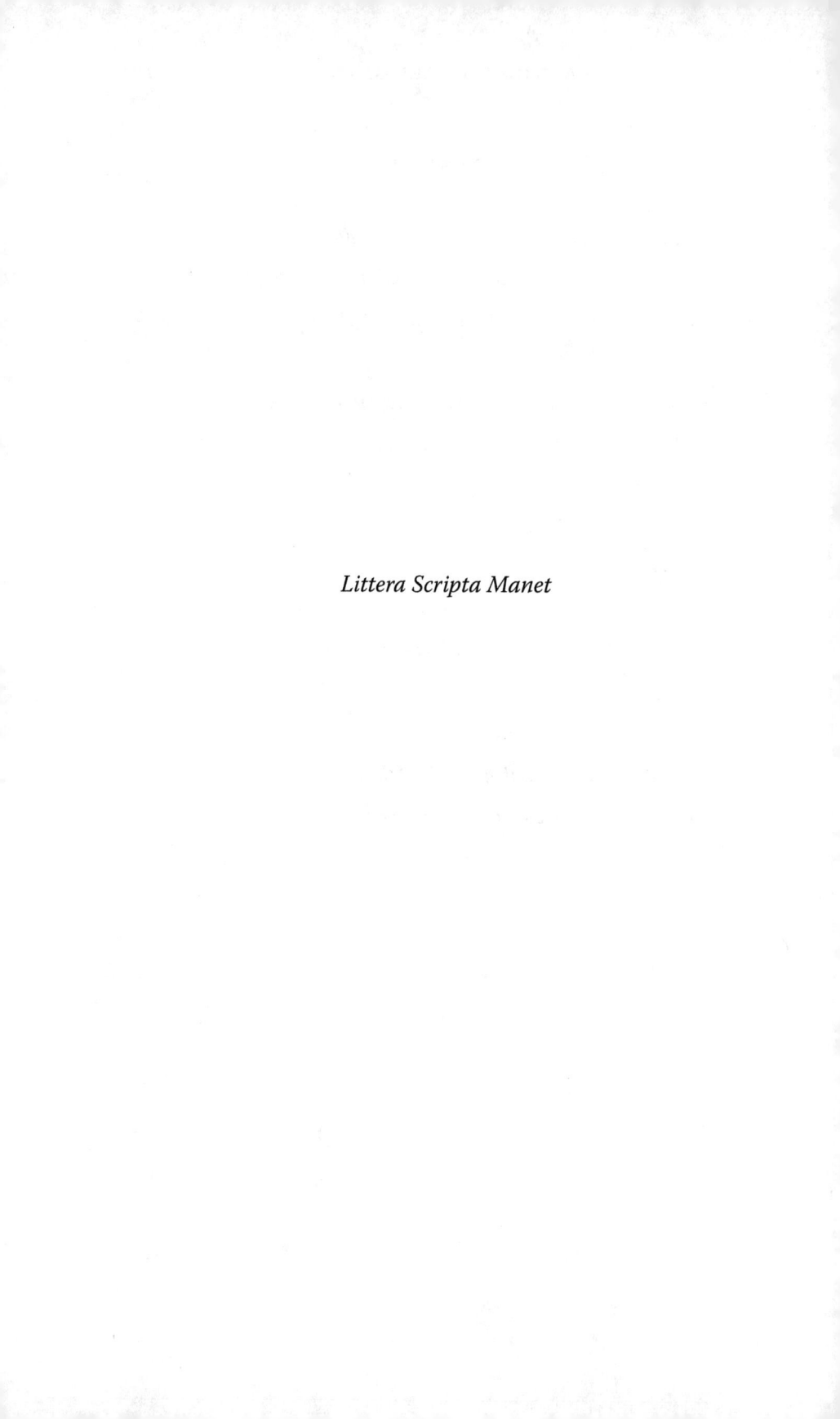

IN MEMORIAM

First Lieutenant Brian McPhillips, 2nd Tanks, 4 April 2003

Corporal Bernard Gooden, 2nd Tanks, 4 April 2003

Lance Corporal Eric Orlowski, 2nd Tanks, 22 March 2003

Lance Corporal Jesus Suarezdelsol, 1st LAR, 30 March 2003

Gunnery Sergeant Joseph Menusa, 1st CEB, 27 March 2003

Sergeant Duane Rios, 1st CEB, 4 April 2003

Second Lieutenant Therrel Childers, 1/5, 21 March 2003

Gunnery Sergeant Jeffery Bohr, 1/5, 10 April 2003

First Sergeant Edward Smith, 2/5, 4 April 2003

Lance Corporal Robert Morgan, 2/5, 27 March 2003

Major Kevin Nave, 3/5, 27 March 2003

Staff Sargent Riayan Tejeda, 3/5, 11 April 2003

Corporal Erik Silva, 3/5, 4 April 2003

Lance Corporal David Owens, 3/5, 11 April 2003

HM3 Michael Johnson, 3/5, 25 March 2003

THE PRESIDENT OF THE UNITED STATES

Takes pleasure in presenting the PRESEDENTIAL UNIT CITATION to I MARINE EXPEDITIONARY FORCE for service as set forth in the following

CITATION:

For extraordinary heroism and outstanding performance in action against enemy forces in support of Operation IRAQI FREEDOM from 21 March to 24 April 2003. During this period, I Marine Expeditionary Force (MEF) (REIN) conducted the longest sequence of coordinated combined army's overland attacks in the history of the Marine Corps.

From the border between Kuwait and Iraq, to the culmination of hostilities north of Baghdad, I MEF advanced nearly 800 kilometers under sustained and heavy combat. Utilizing the devastating combat power of organic aviation assets, coupled with the awesome power resident in the ground combat elements, and maintaining momentum through the Herculean efforts of combat service support elements, I MEF destroyed nine Iraqi Divisions.

This awesome display of combat power was accomplished while simultaneously freeing the Iraqi people from more than 30 years of oppression and reestablishing basic infrastructure in the country. During 33 days of combat, to the transition to civil-military operations, I MEF sustained a tempo of operations never before seen on the modern battlefield, conducting four major river crossings, maintaining initiative, and sustaining forces.

The ferocity and duration of the campaign was made possible through the skills and determination of the Soldiers, Sailors, Airmen, Marines and Coalition Partners comprising I MEF at all levels, all echelons, and in all occupational fields.

By their outstanding courage, aggressive fighting spirit, and untiring devotion to duty, the officers and enlisted personnel of I Marine Expeditionary Force (REIN) reflected great credit upon themselves and upheld the highest traditions of the Marine Corps and the United States Naval Service.

For the President,
/s/ Gordon England
Secretary of the Navy

REGIMENTAL COMBAT TEAM— 5 (REINFORCED)

Headquarters Company, 5th Marines (Reinforced)
Combat Camera Detachment, HQ Bn, 1st Marine Division
Public Affairs Detachment, HQ Bn, 1st Marine Division
Detachment Comm Company, HQ Bn. 1st Marine Division
Regimental Artillery Liaison, HQ Btry, 2nd Bn, 11th Marines
Detachment, H&S Company, 1st CEB
Detachment, H&S Company, 3rd AAV Battalion
Detachment, 1st Radio Battalion (OCE)
Detachment, Intelligence Battalion, I MEF
Detachment, 3rd Civil Affairs Group
Aviation Support Liaison Team 3, MASS-3, 3rd MAW
Detachment, Truck Company, HQ Bn, 4th Marine Division
Detachment, Psychological Operations Company, US Army
RRT, VMU-1, 3rd Marine Aircraft Wing
United Kingdom NBC Decontamination Platoon

1st Battalion, 5th Marines (Reinforced)
Artillery Liaison Team, Battery F, 2nd Bn, 11th Marines
Company C, 3rd AA Battalion
1st Platoon, B Company, 1st CEB
Platoon, 2nd Tanks
Explosive Ordnance Disposal Team

Military Police Team
Human Exploitation Team
NBC detection teams (FOX vehicles)
Detachment, Combat Camera, HQ Bn, 1st Marine Division
UK Explosive Ordinance Disposal/Oil Mitigation Teams
SST, 1st Radio Battalion
Psychological Operations Team

2nd Battalion, 5th Marines (Minus)(Reinforced)
Artillery Liaison Team, Battery F, 2nd Bn, 11th Marines
Company E (-), 3rd AA Battalion
Company B, 2nd Tanks
3rd Platoon, Company B, 1st Combat Engineer Battalion
Human Exploitation Team
NBC detection teams (Fox vehicles)
MEWS team
SST, 1st Radio Battalion
Detachment, Combat Camera, HQ Bn, 1st Marine Division
Psychological Operations Team

3rd Battalion, 5th Marines (Reinforced)
Artillery Liaison Team, Battery K, 3rd Bn, 12th Marines
Company D, 2nd AA Battalion, 2nd Marine Division
Platoon, 2nd Tanks
2nd Platoon, Company B, 1st Combat Engineer Battalion
Explosive Ordinance Disposal Team
Human Exploitation Team
Military Police Team
Explosive Ordinance Disposal/UK Oil Mitigation Teams
SST, 1st Radio Battalion

2nd Tank Battalion (Minus)(Reinforced)
Company A, 2nd Tank Battalion
Company C, 2nd Tank Battalion
Company D, 2nd Tank Battalion
Company F, 2nd Battalion, 5th Marines
Artillery Liaison Team, Battery R, 5th Battalion, 10th Marines

1st Light Armored Recon Battalion (Minus)(Reinforced)
H&S Company
Company C
Company D

Did *Taking Baghdad* make you see war in a new light?
Did it inspire you?
Did it call you to action?

I poured my heart into this work for fifteen years to get it right. So many versions, so much editing went into the artifact you hold in your hands.

So, if it moves you, please leave feedback and give me your thoughts online. The reason I ask, is because leaving comments and good reviews immensely helps the author get his message out. Given the algorithms giants like Amazon, Google, and Barnes and Noble uses, every single review counts to move a book up on their massive competitive marketplace. Please choose any, or all of the online media below to leave feedback.

www.amazon.com, barnesandnoble.com, goodreads.com, google.com, onlinebookclub.org, pluggedin.com

Thank you for your part in helping this book and its message become great.

www.takingbaghdad.com
www.facebook.com/takingbaghdad/

ABOUT THE AUTHOR

Staff Sergeant Aaron Grant retired from the United States Marine Corps in 2008. He served a combat tour with Bravo Company, 2nd Tank Battalion, 2nd Marine Division in Operation Iraqi Freedom. He was a M88-A2 HERCULES crewman in Iraq, a combat correspondent at Camp Pendleton, California, and a combat marksmanship trainer at Quantico, Virginia. He was commander of a local VFW and is commandant of a growing Marine Corps League detachment in his hometown in upstate New York. He is the author of *Shaping the Colonies: Essays on Early American History* and *The Non-Commissioned Officer's War: Combined Action Doctrine that could have Saved Vietnam*. He received his bachelor's degree in American history at Empire State University in 2012. He also holds a master's degree in military history at Norwich University received in 2014. He is a member of Phi Theta Kappa International Honors Society and is a Horatio Alger military scholar. He currently teaches American history using intellectual, economic, and military perspectives at John 15 Leah Homeschooling Group in Naples, NY. Mr. Grant resides in quiet upstate New York with his wife and children.